CREATING NEW CLIENTS

Creating
New Clients

Marketing and selling
professional services

**Kevin Walker,
Cliff Ferguson and
Paul Denvir**

CONTINUUM
London & New York

Continuum
Wellington House
125 Strand, London WC2R 0BB
www.cassell.co.uk

370 Lexington Avenue
New York, NY 10017-6550

First published 1998
Reprinted 1999, 2000

British Library Cataloguing-in-Publication Data
A catalogue record for this book is available from the British Library.

ISBN 0-304-70425-3 (hardback)
      0-8264-5253-1 (paperback)

Designed and typeset by Kenneth Burnley in Irby, Wirral, Cheshire.
Printed and bound in Great Britain by Redwood Books, Trowbridge, Wiltshire.

Contents

Introduction

THE NEED FOR THIS BOOK

Most people study accountancy, law and engineering because they want to graduate into careers as accountants, lawyers and consultants. Very few professionals studied to enter their profession with the desire at the back of their minds to become salespeople. However, as individuals progress in their vocation the nature of work can change. Typically over time professionals become less involved in the technical aspects of doing the job and start to become involved in managing some of the work. Managing involves an interface with the client. This interface often includes the responsibility for the development of on-going work from the client. Further down the career path the responsibility can be extended to seeking new work for the firm. In effect the accountant, lawyer and engineering consultant have 'graduated' into a business development role.

With years of study and practice the tax specialist, architect or technology consultant builds knowledge and skills related to their area of expertise. They understand intimately the processes of their profession. When adopting the new role of business developer for the firm, the professional has to build new knowledge and skills and has to understand a different process. This book is written to help define the most productive selling processes, to build the knowledge of the professional and to clearly delineate the skills required for maximum success in marketing and selling the professional service firm.

Our experience shows us that there are a number of reasons why professionals have to create new clients. It may be because:

*   There has been fee income attrition from the client base. The reasons for this may be within our control. For example, the last piece of work for a client could have been perceived to have provided poor value. On the other hand the attrition can be for reasons beyond our control. Perhaps a take-over has meant that the acquiring organisation's advisers have taken our client.

- The nature of some work is transactional and non-recurring – for instance much Corporate Finance work. This means there is a constant need to develop new clients.

- The firm has ambitious growth targets and the best predictions of income from on-going and new work from current clients will not hit the target figure. New clients have to be found.

- Firms decide to enter new markets they have never been involved in previously. By definition the client base is zero. The only way forward is to create new clients.

- Promotion to senior positions in some firms is dependent on the professional being a proven business developer. This may mean that the professional has to demonstrate an ability to win new work from non-clients.

We have met very few professionals who get involved in creating new clients because it is a first-choice activity for them. It is an activity which *has* to be carried out. Nonetheless the reasons driving the creation of new clients are impelling and the successful management of this process is vital to firms who seek to grow their business.

WHAT THIS BOOK IS AND ISN'T ABOUT

If someone asked us the smartest way to increase fee income next year we would not answer, 'Go out and create some new clients.' In most situations this would be poor advice. Our guidance would typically be as follows:

1. Get close to your existing clients and ensure that work which *should* be captive, *is* captive. Guarantee ownership of any recurring work.

2. Look for new opportunities within your existing clients to help them with your expertise. It is far easier, quicker and cheaper to sell to existing clients than to create new clients.

3. Encourage your existing clients to provide you with referrals and introductions to other parts of their organisation (where you do not currently get work) or to other prospective clients whom they know.

4. You need still more work? OK, go on and create new clients.

We could easily have chosen to write this book on subjects 1, 2 and 3. After all, for most firms over 90 per cent of next year's income will be derived from these sources. One day we will write such a book. However, this book is exclusively focused on the fourth process.

We have not selected this as the most important process – clearly for most firms it cannot be. It must be more important to secure 90 per cent of the income, not 10 per cent. This fourth process, though, is seen by most people in professional firms as being the most difficult and the one which appears to be most foreign to their natural instincts. That is why this book is about creating new clients.

WHAT IS THE DIFFERENCE BETWEEN THIS BOOK AND ANY OTHER BOOK ON THE SUBJECT OF SELLING?

As the authors of this book we have spent over sixty years between us working in selling, sales management and marketing. We continue as practitioners of these skills within our own business. In the last ten years we have all spent a high proportion of our time working with professional firms – Big 6 firms, 'second tier' accountancy firms, lawyers, specialist consultancies, consulting engineers, architects and so on.

What we have not tried to do is to shoehorn practices which sit comfortably in say, the FMCG (Fast Moving Consumer Goods) business, into the professional services market. There is a very big difference between selling a product and selling a business-to-business professional service. The buying and selling of professional services is special because:

- The professional is very often (literally) selling himself. Chemistry and trust are much more important factors in the decision to buy.

- The decision to buy often involves a decision to confide business-critical information to a third party. Such buying decisions are not taken lightly.

- The decision to buy from a professional services firm can mean a long-term commitment. Some professional services are short term and transactional but most are purchased with the intention of a long and on-going relationship.

- The selling process in most professional firms is carried out by people whose primary role and training is in another field of expertise – their profession.

- When the professional service is sold, the professional then has to put on a different hat and become the creator and provider of the service. (Imagine a computer salesman having to go back to the factory to assemble the computers he sold the day before!) This means that the marketing and selling of professional services can become sporadic. One cannot be out selling while assembling computers on the production line. This is a recognised constraint when selling professional services.

This authors of this book recognise all of the above scenarios. They represent the starting point for us.

Having spent so much of our time working with engineering consultancies, law firms, accountancy practices (both large and smaller) and consultants of all types, we know that these businesses are different from each other. However, we believe that, in many ways, the commonalities outweigh the differences.

This is implicitly recognised today by the growth of both national and regional organisations which aim to improve professional services marketing. They attract members from every corner of the professional market. For this reason we are confident that the content of this book has application and value to anyone who is selling their expertise in this highly competitive field.

WHY PROFESSIONALS ARE UNCOMFORTABLE WITH SELLING AND FACE-TO-FACE MARKETING ACTIVITIES

The image of selling and face-to-face marketing

For many professionals the image of selling sits poorly with their self-image.

Selling is often personified by the 'foot in the door' and 'I'll stay here until you sign' approach, which is associated (rightly or wrongly) with the archetypal double-glazing salesperson.

Other images which spring easily to mind are the techniques of harassment and spurious incentives employed by timeshare merchants.

Stories of gullible people being sold unsuitable pensions and other financial products also reach the newspapers on a regular basis.

There is nothing wrong with buying double glazing or deciding that timeshare is an excellent way to organise holidays. Pensions and financial protection are excellent concepts. What is wrong is not the product or service – it is the intent with which the sellers approach their potential buyers. The products in themselves are totally amoral. It is the approach of the sales people which reflects morality or immorality. Lying and putting people under pressure in order to sell them something is immoral whatever the product or service being sold. Putting one's personal well-being and the health of one's own organisation before the well-being of the client is poor selling – no matter who you are and what your organisation produces.

All products and services can be sold morally, if people have the integrity and values to approach the selling and buying process from an ethical standpoint. We have made every effort in this book to do just this in our approach to the marketing and selling of professional services. If you are looking for 'tricks' and short-cuts to get people to commit to your services when they don't really need them, put this book down now.

If you want to know how to win new clients using totally professional and ethical methods, this book is for you. Good selling practice is totally consistent with ethical practice.

Professionals have a particular fear of failure

Professionals give advice. They spend their lives being paid to be right. This is the nature of most professional work. Professionals are not used to being wrong, and being wrong is anathema to them. In his *Harvard Business Review* article, 'Teaching Smart People How to Learn', Chris Argyris publishes his research conclusions on why professionals can find learning more difficult. Argyris says, 'People who rarely experience failure end up not knowing how to deal with it effectively.'

Essentially, if we are always used to being right we find it very difficult to accept that we can be wrong. The tendency is to defend our actions – not admit that we have erred in judgement.

Selling and marketing are not exact sciences and we will never make all of our efforts work perfectly all of the time. There is going to be failure. All selling and marketing is partially a 'numbers game'. Not every prospect becomes a client. Not every selling meeting identifies work opportunities. Not every proposal wins.

This reality can have two negative effects:

*   Some professionals avoid selling and marketing work where the chances of failure are highest (and selling to win new clients is definitely in this category). Thereby they avoid the pain of failure.

*   Professionals are not open to examination of the way they have conducted a selling process to a client. Losing will be ascribed to either dirty tricks from competitors, stupid clients or uncontrollable factors. Any shortcomings passing these hurdles will then be rationalised away. Many will not have their management of the selling process candidly examined and criticised. In this way they avoid the pain of failure.

There is only one answer to this problem. When engaged in marketing and selling activities we have to discard the benchmarks which serve us well in assessing our professional performance. They are not relevant to assessing our performance in the processes of creating new clients. We are not suggesting accepting lower benchmarks – we are advocating totally different benchmarks. This is a different activity, a different process and different measures of performance are required.

OUR APPROACH

Practical, not theoretical

We have an intense interest in things which *really* work. Put another way, we are not interested in clever theory which will not stand the rigours of application in the field. This book is a real nuts and bolts 'How to' publication.

Much of what we have included has been learned through direct first-hand experience – selling our own capabilities and expertise. However, we are not averse to learning from others. We pick up ideas through our own reading, we learn from training and we learn from the experiences which our clients relate to us. What we have included in this book is the distillation of best practice we have accumulated in our careers to date.

Will we learn more? Will we improve and add to our ideas? We certainly hope so. This is intended to be an authoritative word on the subject – not the last word.

Examples and illustrations

In many places in the text we have given examples of dialogue. There are some points to bear in mind regarding these illustrations.

- These examples are given in order to bring the 'theory' to life.

- They are probably not the words that you may choose to use.

- We are not claiming that this is the only way the dialogue could develop.

In all our training we stress that we are not trying to change people's personalities. What we are attempting to do is to encourage participants to apply certain skills and practices, using their own personality to project these. We would encourage readers likewise.

Gender distinctions

For simplicity we have decided to be politically incorrect. In all instances when we refer to the professional this person will be male. When we refer to the client this person will always be female. This saves a multiplicity of he/shes and his/hers.

References

The following works are referred to in the text:

'Teaching Smart People How to Learn' by Chris Argyris (*Harvard Business Review*, May/June 1997).

Personal Selling Strategies for Consultants and Professionals by Richard Carlson (John Wiley and Sons).

'How Clients Choose' by David Maister (from *Managing the Professional Service Firm*, Free Press).

Marketing Warfare and *Positioning* by Al Ries and Jack Trout (McGraw-Hill).

Section 1 The PACE Pipeline

Chapter 1 **Introducing the PACE Pipeline**

WHAT IS THE PACE PIPELINE?

The PACE Pipeline model acts as a framework for this book. The model enables us to:

- Identify those actions which will ensure a flow of work from both existing and new clients.
- Plan and manage in a balanced way the activities which are required to stimulate this flow.

What exactly is the PACE Pipeline? How do we define it?

● ●

Definition:

The opportunities for future business flow generated by accumulated efforts and activities.

● ●

Let us take an example. Two people are talking and one says to the other: 'Paul's pipeline is looking really good.' The speaker has calculated, using some measure or other, that Paul is in a strong position to win a lot of work in the foreseeable future. The reason this has occurred has something to do with a combination of efforts which Paul (or his predecessors) have carried out.

Similarly if someone is viewed as having a weak pipeline, the opportunities for business on the horizon are looking poor. Even if this second person has had extremely good business development performance in the past, the future is not looking good. Pipeline is all about activity management today which will determine our success in the future.

WILL THE PACE PIPELINE HELP US?

The first question which many people (rightly) raise when they see a concept or model is: 'Will this apply to our business? Is this one of those "theories" which is OK for people selling baked beans but has no application to the world of selling professional services?'

The model will be useful if the following conditions apply to your marketplace:

1. *There is a time lag between activities being devoted to business development and the results of that effort* (i.e. the successful winning of that work).

   Judge this from your own experience. To us it is an everyday occurrence for professionals to relate stories of spending two years or more in the pursuit of a new client before winning the first piece of work. Is yours an instant business?

2. *Not all business development activity produces results.*

   Does every one of your selling visits to clients and prospective clients end in some form of work? Do you have a 100 per cent conversion of proposals to business?

3. *Results cannot be guaranteed.*

   Is there anyone out there who is willing to guarantee that their business development results will be on (or over) target next year?

4. *Activities can be planned, managed and monitored* (in a way that results cannot).

MANAGING ACTIVITY

Most firms still try to manage by results. What do we mean by this? Engage someone who has responsibility for business development within a professional services firm in a conversation. Ask questions like, 'How is business development going? What's the picture like? How are we doing? Can we look at the numbers?'

The chances are that when the numbers are produced, these will relate to the results which the firm has produced to date. It will include the work already done and invoiced and the work booked and confirmed but not yet carried out. Good, bad or indifferent, there is nothing which can be done to change the figures. If they are bad perhaps the senior partner will exhort everyone to sell harder but this is likely to have little impact.

Wear, for a moment, the hat of a Production Management Consultant. You are visiting a factory which you know has poor quality output. When you go down on the shop floor the factory quality manager tells you that he knows exactly how many rejects per thousand he has and he knows exactly in which batches they occur. You ask him how he knows this. He takes you to the end of the production line and introduces you to his quality team. They measure every aspect of the quality of the product as it rolls off the line.

This factory manager has totally misunderstood his role as the manager of quality. His job is to improve quality, not just measure it. While he and his team focus on the output and not the input, they are bystanders – not managers. Sure, having the output data is helpful. It tells us if any changes we made earlier have worked or not – but it is not enough.

If the only measures we have in place are on the quality and quantity of output, then we are not in control of production in the future. Measures need to be in place to ensure that the quality and quantity of inputs are also right.

What about the factory manager who has high quality output but once again regards his role as one of measurement? If quality is good is there any need for him to change his way of working? This person should not sleep too comfortably in his bed. Even if production is good today, this individual will never know if an input of raw materials is below specification and he will never spot the new operative setting the machines at unacceptable tolerances. Eventually the poor quality inputs will work their way through to the outputs – with consequent negative effects.

This scenario is pure fantasy. No one would manage a production facility in this way.

The acid test of Pipeline management

Despite management being about the planning and control of inputs, our conclusion is that in most professional services firms this principle has not been translated into the way business development is managed. Sometimes people deny this accusation. To clarify the real position we need to apply the acid test.

Marketing Consultant	Show me all the figures and statistics you have on work sold to clients. (Outputs.)
Response	Printouts, charts and statistics are produced.
Marketing Consultant	Now show me the information on the activities which will produce your income stream of the future. (Inputs.)
Response	Nothing much is produced. A seminar was run last week and it is thought that four people went along to talk to the clients.

There is nothing in this example to ensure a restful night for the senior people in the firm. The business may be great today, but the results in six or nine months' time appear to be left to chance.

That's the acid test.

Managers need information to enable them to make their management decisions. A firm without an accurate measurement of the inputs into business development is running a risk. How does one manage anything without data? How meaningful is that data without an original plan to compare it against?

Conclusion

If we are going to measure not only business development *results* but also business development *activity*, this suggests two things:

1. We should have a plan for business development activity – in that way we are measuring against some form of benchmark.

2. We need to understand the different activities which will produce results.

THE MODEL

The PACE Pipeline model provides a simple and graphic way of identifying the business development activities in which we can engage and the potential sources of business where these activities can be applied.

Figure 1.1:   The PACE Pipeline model

Everything which lies within the circle of the Pipeline we consider to be our Total Defined Market. We will return to this definition later.

The flow of future business is going to emanate from five potential sources. These are:

Current clients (P4)

Our role here is one of *Protecting.* We must:

- Execute today's work exceptionally well.
- Deliver an unbeatable service, support and contact package to our best clients to protect them from competitive incursion.
- Sell existing and new capabilities to them.

Defined Prospects with whom we are in dialogue (P3)

These are potential clients with whom we are talking about business issues. We are in the process of trying to find mutually acceptable ways in which our firm may be able to support them in dealing with some of these issues. We are *Projecting* that at some point in the future they will do work with us (some will, some will not).

Defined Prospects to whom we are carrying out marketing activities but with whom we are not in dialogue (P2)

These people may receive regular mailings from us, they may be invited to our seminars and round tables, they may even participate in some of our corporate entertainment – but we have not had the opportunity of sitting down with a senior decision-maker and talking about business – her business and our business. We are in the process of *Promoting* ourselves.

Defined Prospects not yet marketed to (P1)

This Segment of the Pipeline *does not* represent all other people and organisations not represented in P2, P3 or P4. In P1 are prospective clients we have consciously *chosen* to focus on.

If we are to market ourselves to prospective clients with a view to meeting with them and eventually doing work with them, it is a logical conclusion that we should decide whom we would wish to become our clients. We examine this process in detail in Section 2. This process is defined as *Prospecting.*

The market

There could be people and organisations who are just names to us today, who may provide us with work in the future. These people live outside the circle of our Pipeline. We cannot trust to luck that they will knock on our door. If we are going to be in control of our destiny and future client base we need to invest time and effort into defining the best of these prospects (P1) in order that we can initiate our approach toward them, and by doing so bring them into the Promoting (P2) Segment of the Pipeline.

What lies inside the Pipeline are, therefore, only those people and organisations who are *defined* to us, hence the expression *Total Defined Market*

Applications

The PACE Pipeline can be used in a number of different dimensions. It can be used as a basis for examining and planning a whole firm's future business prospects, it can be used for a team or department within a firm, it can be used by an individual. It can even be used if the firm has (and always will have) only one client.

An example

As an example, let us take a practice area within a professional services firm for which we may be responsible. This practice area has a total income objective for the year.

Planning P4 activity

Before the year begins, the team needs to sit down and calculate, to the best of its knowledge, how much business can be derived from existing clients. This is an accumulation of on-going work, repeat work, job extensions and new work. A plan is needed to define the activities required to convert this potential business into work.

Almost inevitably the volume of business to be derived from existing clients (P4 Segment) is not going to fulfil the entire income budget. Even if it will for this year, it is highly unlikely that the firm can survive for ever on its existing client base.

Planning P3 activity

The next step is to look at what lies in the Projecting Segment (P3). In this Segment of the Pipeline there may be prospects who are about to confirm work for the first time in the very near future; there will also be people whom we have only just met, and there will be people and organisations which fall between these two extremes.

The quality and quantity of the Defined Prospects and the quality of our selling process will determine the levels of new income we are likely to generate in the next twelve months from the P3 Segment. We next need to plan the activities required to convert as much of these P3 business opportunities as possible.

Planning P2 to P3 activity

Given that only a percentage of the P3 prospects will convert into clients, we need to bring more Defined Prospects into the P3 Segment from P2. We therefore must identify which of these Defined Prospects we wish to be proactive in approaching with the aim of initiating face-to-face meetings. The next step is to formulate a plan of action as to how we are going to do this.

Planning P2 activity

In order that we can, in future months and years, dip back into a 'warm' pool of P2 Defined Prospects we need to plan the marketing activities which will keep our name in front of Defined Prospects. We need these people to be aware of us, to know what we do and to know how well we do it. With luck, some of the organisations in this pool will respond to our marketing efforts and ring us, but we should not write cheques on the basis of this happening.

Planning P1 activity

The P2 pool needs to be examined and 'topped up' from P1 regularly. We should look at the organisations we have defined in P2 and ask the question: 'Are these still the best prospects for our attentions or should we drop some of them and add others?' The pool will deplete over a period in any case. If we are being successful we will be moving Defined Prospects from P2 into P3 and many (hopefully) of these into P4. We therefore need to plan the activity which is required to find those organisations most closely resembling the 'ideal client' of the future – bringing them from the undefined market and into our P1 Segment.

Pipeline management or rowing boat management?

The word which repeats again and again is the word 'activity'.

This is what Pipeline management is all about. Look at the definition again. Managing the Pipeline is about managing the opportunities for future business flow. This is achieved through planning and managing the totality of the business development activities. Pipeline management is about managing inputs.

One cannot manage outputs or results. We call this 'rowing boat management'. In this type of craft the person rowing is going forward (they hope) but their only view is backward. All their inputs tell them where they have gone, not where they are going.

GROWING THE BUSINESS BY MANAGING THE PIPELINE

In order to grow our businesses in the future we need to do just five things well *concurrently*. These are depicted on our Pipeline model on page 10.

1. *Select the best Defined Prospects.*

   This is the focus of Section 2, Chapter 2.

2. *Begin and maintain an effective marketing contact campaign with these Defined Prospects.*

   We examine best practice in this area in Section 2, Chapter 3.

3. *Find an opportunity to create a face-to-face dialogue with key people within Defined Prospects.*

   In Section 2, Chapter 4 we look at how to use the telephone to make appointments with prospective clients.

   In Sections 3 and 4 we examine in detail the attributes, skills and processes needed to turn that potentially adrenaline-pumping first meeting into the beginning of a selling (and buying!) process.

Figure 1.2:   Managing the PACE Pipeline

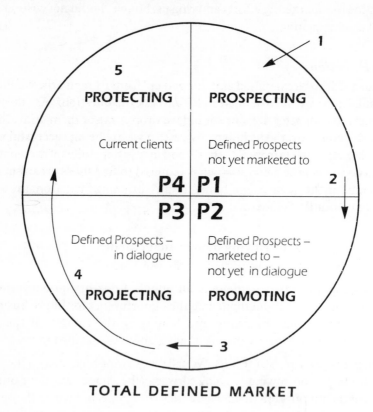

TOTAL DEFINED MARKET

4.   *Manage the selling process effectively and use tactics which are likely to result in a new client – not a wasted sales process.*

In Section 5 we consider the most successful proven ways of pursuing the selling process and also highlight commonly employed unsuccessful tactics.

5.   *Protect our existing clients from competitive incursion and continue to secure work from them.*

This subject is so important that we decided to devote a separate title to it.

TRAPS IN PIPELINE MANAGEMENT

We continually see two common problems which stem from a lack of detailed management of the Pipeline. These problems result in the firm or individual experiencing the roller coaster ride of 'feast and famine'. The problems are so endemic that many professionals come to the conclusion that big swings in business levels are impossible to avoid. Fortunately this is not true – avoid the following traps and we will avoid the dangerous implications of the 'feast and famine' cycle.

Trap 1: The implications of the mix of activity are not considered.

Take the case of a team who, when examining their Pipeline for the next year, come to the conclusion that their objectives can be met by working with their existing clients plus bringing on board four big new clients. When the team looks at its P3 Projecting Segment it finds that it has six major prospects which have distinct possibilities of being converted within the next year.

The team puts all its efforts into converting these opportunities. The selling and contact campaigns are worked out and co-ordinated, and everyone puts in maximum effort. By the second half of the year, four have been won and it is clear that in the other two cases there is no prospect of winning work in the short term. Two out of three is not bad. The question is, from where will the new business come in Year 2?

Twelve months on, when the team is considering its business development plans for Year 2, it is looking at an empty P3 Segment. The team also recognises one of the underpinning principles of the Pipeline concept – that there is a time lag between activities being devoted to business development and the results of that effort. Twelve months may not be long enough to bring prospects through from the P2 Segment to becoming clients. Even if the team could be successful in this task, success will probably happen towards the end of Year 2 and will have little impact on Year 2 income.

Again, this scenario is working on the assumption that the team has a healthy P2 Segment – lots of interesting-looking Defined Prospects who have been kept warm through good marketing efforts. Did that happen in Year 1 or was that one of the casualties of the big push to convert the six?

During Year 1 when the big push was under way, was effort also put into updating the quality and quantity of prospects considered 'Defined' – as a feeder for the P2 Segment?

There needs to be a balance of activity put into the different segments of the Pipeline if we are to control the flow of business in both the short and long term. There is no standard formula which can be applied. Each firm needs to consider its situation and decide how that balance of activity should be apportioned. Some activity needs to be exerted into *all* Segments of the Pipeline. The firm then has to ensure that individuals are responsible and accountable for those activities which will generate the business flow which the organisation requires.

Trap 2: People become victims of their own success – too busy or too complacent.

This is a very common scenario. Figure 1.3 (page 12) depicts what happens. Let us take the scenario of a professional given a clear field to develop new business. The horizontal axis represents time, the vertical axis measures the level of activity and the level of results.

Figure 1.3: Unmanaged pipeline activity and ensuing results

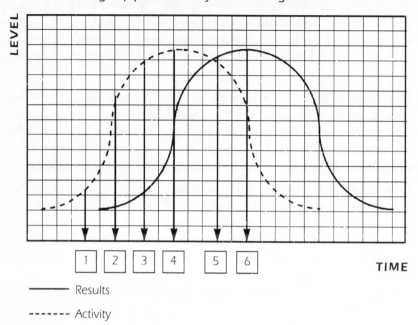

——— Results

------- Activity

For a period of time the professional puts in effort and produces no results (Timeline Point 1). This is the Pipeline timelag principle manifesting itself again.

In this scenario the level of effort put into selling and marketing then increases quite sharply. Perhaps the person has completed some professional work and more of his effort is business development orientated, perhaps he is concerned with a lack of early success and decides to work even harder. There could be a number of factors influencing this increase in activity.

However, if we look at the Timeline Point 2, the results are disappointing. Most people in the firm will only be aware of this aspect of the campaign. After all, the systems only measure results. It could even be at this point that someone senior decides to 'pull the plug'. There have been many months of effort and very little success to show for it.

At Timeline Point 3 we see increasing results coming through and the effort is very high. At Timeline Point 4 the results are definitely looking good and the activity has peaked. At this point in time the professional has generated an extremely good Pipeline but he is working fourteen hours a day, six days a week on his quest. This cannot continue and it is only natural that the activity dips from this peak.

At Timeline Point 5 the activity has clearly dropped but interestingly the results continue to climb. One reason for this phenomenon is particularly common to professional services firms. Professional staff are most often not only responsible for generating the income but are also involved in the design and delivery of the 'product'. The more work won, the less time there is for marketing and business development.

At Timeline Point 6, results are at their zenith but business development activity has dropped away considerably. This effort level has no immediate impact on business levels – but it will. The only question is 'When?'

So what should the professional do at Timeline Point 6? He could work harder, reduce his own chargeable work, recruit more resources and through these efforts build up his selling activity to generate more opportunities. However, even if he were to do this the results of this second wave of activity may not generate business before the results curve dips alarmingly. The time to redirect activity is at Timeline Point 3 or 4, on the basis of future business (the Pipeline), not past results. In fact Timeline Point 6 is the worst time to recruit new resources – i.e. in advance of a dip in business. We may be recruiting for redundancy.

The trap occurs because the only visible line in many firms is the results curve, therefore decisions are made on this information. Remember – results can lie! The key is to make the dotted line visible and manage it well – i.e. manage the Pipeline, as well as the results it brings.

**Managing the Pipeline is the basis
of managing business development.**

Section 2 **Getting to the First Meeting**

Chapter 2 **Defining the Best Prospects**

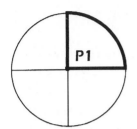

The Need to have a Process
Trigger Factors
Filter Factors
Using Trigger and Filter Selection Criteria
Researching for Triggers and Filters Match
Treating Defined Prospects as Clients

THE NEED TO HAVE A PROCESS

The acid test of Prospect Definition

Assume we have been given the task of creating a client base starting with only a blank piece of paper. Where will we start? Clearly we are going to have to sell our services to prospective clients. But which prospective clients?

An acid test of how well organised a firm is in relation to the generation of new business income, lies in its answers to the questions:

- Who are your Defined Prospects?

- Who are the people or organisations whom you would like to become clients in the future?

- What criteria did you use to define these prospects?

We have found many firms who do not have any meaningful list of Defined Prospects. They may carry out some broad-brush marketing in the hope that some potential clients will surrender themselves up but they have never worked on the detail of exactly which organisations they would like to have as clients at some point in the future.

GIGO

Quite clearly, if we are not concerned about the types of prospects who populate Segment 1 of the PACE Pipeline, then by default we are not concerned with the eventual client base we deal with on a day-to-day basis.

This is known as the GIGO principle – Garbage In, Garbage Out.

In the same way if we *are* selective of the prospects who populate Segment 1 of the PACE Pipeline, but we use inappropriate selection criteria, the GIGO principle will again work. If we select the 'wrong' prospects then we end up with an unsatisfactory outcome from our prospecting work. An 'unsatisfactory outcome' can mean one of two things:

1. It could mean that the Defined Prospects we identify in Segment 1 eventually become clients but in the fullness of time we wish they had not.

    There are clients who are poor payers. There are clients who are so demanding that every piece of work becomes an unprofitable chore. There are clients who negotiate over every penny and will not pay the going rate for the work to be carried out. There are clients whose type of work is not really in our main line of expertise.

    If we have a client base populated with too many of these types of clients we need to go back and take a close look at our prospect selection criteria (if we have any).

2. It could also mean that the prospects we have chosen never make the journey to the latter stages of Segment 3, crossing the threshold into Segment 4 and becoming our clients. That is, we could have selected prospects whom it is difficult or impossible to convert.

When selecting those prospects from the marketplace whom we wish to include as our Defined Prospects we need to consider both of these aspects – are they of the right 'calibre' and are they 'winnable'?

When we do get an answer to the question, 'What criteria did you use to define these prospects?' we get mixed responses. We typically get answers such as:

*   They are all within close proximity to our offices.
*   They are big organisations. We figure they must have a lot of potential.
*   They are big spenders on our type of work.
*   We know someone in this company.
*   They are in a market in which we are comfortable or where we have expertise.

If the question does elicit a response, then most often one of these reasons is given. There may be two, but this is rare. Three is extremely rare. There is nothing wrong with any of the above answers but in isolation – or even in tandem – they are not enough to identify truly a Defined Prospect.

Why are professionals appointed?

Why does a senior manager of an organisation decide to appoint a professional services firm? Does he wake up one morning, draw back the curtains and think, 'What a wonderful day; I think I'll wear that bright new tie the children bought me for my birthday and . . . I think I'll appoint a new firm of solicitors this afternoon. That'll give me something to do.'

Of course the suggestion is quite ridiculous. Most organisations would prefer never to appoint professionals. At times we can justify our fees as an *investment* which the client is making, but on most occasions clients regard our fees as costs. What organisation wants to incur more costs than it has to?

When professionals are appointed it is usually because the client has no real option. The client needs to do something and the client's organisation does not have the capability to do this something with the internal resources which it possesses. For example:

- Clients have to take specialist advice when there are changes to complex VAT legislation which may affect them.

- Clients have to have professional surveying advice when they are expanding their production premises.

- Clients have to take advice when they are involved in employment law litigation.

TRIGGER FACTORS

What may be bad news to a prospective client can be good news to a professional services provider. The three situations outlined above are examples of what we call Triggers. Triggers are the situations which occur which cause an organisation to consider the use of outside professional advice. They literally *trigger* the need.

In the vast majority of occasions Triggers are events over which the prospective professional services provider has no control. Indeed in most situations, the potential client has no control of them: they are caused by factors external to the client. When they occur however, a chain of events begins to unfold. One part of this chain is the appointment of professional advisers.

This may result in the incumbent advisers being appointed. However, if there is ever a time when a client will consider other options, it is at the time when a new Trigger occurs. If the incumbents have provided good advice and service in the past, they are in a good position to be re-appointed. However if a viable alternative is also in the wings, it is likely that a prudent organisation will consider a second or third option – even when the decision to appoint needs to be made quite quickly. If it is a 'bushfire' situation, expect the incumbents to be re-appointed. That is usually the safest bet.

The basic guideline for winning new business from prospective clients is:

No Trigger, no opportunity.

Examples of Triggers

Typical Triggers could be:

An organisation is known to be acquisitive.
The likelihood is that this will continue. Acquisitions, mergers and disposals create lots of work for professionals.

A company is operating in a market subject to fast-changing technology.
Such companies have to make many changes in the way they operate – sometimes very quickly. They may have to re-invest in equipment. They may have to develop and change their product lines. They may need advice on how to introduce and manage new technology.

An organisation is subject to changes in legislation and regulations.

Compliance to the new laws may mean changes in operating procedures, it may mean new investment, it may mean new employment terms and contracts, it may mean new reward systems.

A company is subjected to high competitive pressures.

The introduction of different competing processes or new competition from low-cost Third World countries may mean that a company has to find new and better ways of organising itself, reducing costs and becoming more efficient.

There is a change of people at the top of the organisation.

New appointees will often want to stamp their authority on an organisation by reviewing completely the advice sources it uses from the outside. This is nearly always seen as a threat when we are on the receiving end. We should also consider it an opportunity when it is happening to one of our competitors incumbent in an interesting prospect.

An organisation is having changes within the workforce.

Both recruitment and downsizing provide opportunities for professionals. Companies with high staff turnover can also be a source of work.

The organisation is growing.

The faster growing the organisation, the greater the opportunities. Growing organisations have people to recruit and train, they have new practices to install, they need to build and relocate, they need new technology systems to compete, they enter new markets in which they need guidance and advice. All provide opportunities for professionals.

The organisation has had a poor experience or poor advice from its current advisers.

An organisation may have retained a law firm for thirty years. The most likely time it thinks about 'taking the risk' of finding new lawyers is when the risk seems least. If the client now perceives she is receiving poor service or advice, then she perceives little risk in considering a change.

There is one word which sits behind all Triggers. That is the word 'change'. Organisations which are subject to change – whatever its cause – provide more opportunities for professional services providers. The type and intensity of change will determine how 'Trigger rich' a Defined Prospect could be. The professional who is talking with organisations which are likely candidates for significant change is the professional who is best positioned to win new clients.

Does this mean that if we select organisations which look 'Trigger rich' we will have success in selecting the best Defined Prospects? Not necessarily, we do need to consider some other factors. These factors we call the Filters.

FILTER FACTORS

A Filter is a criterion which either:

- Indicates that a prospect may be easier (or more difficult) to approach.

- Indicates that a prospect may be more interesting (or less interesting) than other potential prospects we may consider.

There are many potential Filters which can be considered. The typical answers we receive to the question, 'What criteria did you use to define these prospects?' are all examples of Filters.

Examples of Filters which indicate that a prospect could be easier to approach

Prospects where we know people.

These will usually be easier to penetrate. The higher the position of our contacts the better.

Prospects where we can potentially get an introduction.

If we know their banker and we have a track record of reciprocity, then we have a better potential opportunity.

Prospects where the incumbent professional's expertise would seem inappropriate to the type and size of client concerned.

The most common example of this is the company which started small, appointed small local advisers and has now grown to the size where the capabilities of the advisers are stretched (if not exceeded).

Prospects where the likely services they would use are a good match for the capabilities we can provide.

There is little point approaching a large potential client if much of the client's fee producing work is likely to be in a niche in which we have no specific expertise.

Prospects where the decision-making process is likely to be tangible and influenceable.

Some professionals we have worked with choose not to approach prospects where they know the ultimate decision-makers reside outside of the UK and/or are not contactable. This decision is usually based on sound (and often painful) experience.

Prospects operating in a market where we have a track record and credibility.

Too many professionals are of the opinion that 'advice is advice – it doesn't matter if the client is a widget manufacturer or a travel agent – it can all be applied'. Clearly it doesn't matter to the professionals who think this way. However, in our experience and the experience of the thousands of other professionals with whom we have worked, it does matter to most clients.

When we meet a prospective client face-to-face for the first time, like it or not, that person is going to be making judgements about our *capability, credibility* and *compatibility.*

Most clients want advisers who understand *their* business – not necessarily their organisation (at least not straight away) – but certainly their industry or market. In a one-hour initial meeting it is all but impossible to hide a lack of such understanding and knowledge. We have had professionals dispute this. However, if you ask these professionals if it would be possible for someone who knew little about their business to bluff his way through a one-hour business meeting with them and not be 'discovered', their original premise is severely challenged.

Our real understanding of the prospect's business comes through in the words and terminologies we use, it comes through in the questions we ask (and don't ask), it comes through in the conclusions we are able to draw from the information with which the prospective client provides us. We should be very certain that the other person will have a good understanding of what we know about their type of business at the end of one hour.

We must also realise that in this scenario we are being benchmarked. If the incumbent provider is doing a reasonable job and if they have been installed for any length of time, they will have the advantage of knowing the client's business. If the client finishes the initial meeting with the thought, 'Well he's probably a good solicitor in terms of employment law and litigation but he clearly knows nothing about the international freight forwarding market', this may be reason enough to stick with the incumbent advisers.

We have seen example after example of individuals particularly successful in the generation of new clients who have a specific knowledge of, and credibility within, a market sector.

● ●

The Market Specialist – a Case Study

One illustration of the market specialist which comes to mind, was a consultant who was working within a small team of IT experts focused on providing consultancy in communications and office systems.

The whole team was struggling to meet its expected targets with the exception of this one individual. He had more work than he could handle. He had no trouble in meeting new prospects and he had no problem in winning work from them. His secret? He had trained to become a solicitor. He had begun work with a firm but realised that this was not what he wanted to do. Somehow he ended up in IT consultancy.

Knowing the workings, shortcomings and most importantly the mindset of solicitors, he focused all his efforts into this sector. He was comfortable with law firms, they with him. They were not faced with the prospect of having to educate him before really meaningful dialogue about their office systems requirements could take place.

One example. We have lots more.

● ●

Selecting a target market?

There could be a number of criteria which could cause us to focus on a particular market (or two).

These include:

- A market or industry which is subject to continual external forces which drives the need for new or outside expertise. (A sort of macro Trigger.)

- A market or industry where we have a recent and valued track record.

- A market with high growth potential.

- A market or industry which is seen to be less fee sensitive.

- A market or industry in which our competitors are seen to carry out very profitable work.

- A market or industry which we see as very stimulating or personally developmental to work in.

Becoming a market specialist

To become a market specialist we need to build a knowledge of:

- The critical success factors for organisations in this market.

- Benchmarks which demonstrate success for players in this market.

- The changes, pressures and opportunities faced by players in this market.

This involves on-going exposure to organisations in the chosen market arena plus the study of key 'trade' publications. A regular subscription to these journals can keep us abreast of current and impending events (Triggers?) which may be affecting (or about to affect) potential Defined Prospects.

Examples of Filters which indicate that a prospect could be more interesting to approach

The financial resilience of the prospect.

We have seen organisations take this as a 'default' filter. In other words, if the prospect does not look financially resilient in the long term, it should not be considered.

Financially resilient does not necessarily mean profitable. It was not so long ago in our memories that the UK clearing banks all made losses. This dip in their fortunes did not consign them to the waste heap of prospects for professional services providers. A downturn in profitability in a financially resilient organisation may be an indication of Triggers impacting upon the business. Triggers mean work.

The size of the prospect.

Size can be measured in many ways. It could be the turnover of the organisation. It could be the total headcount. It could be the headcount in one particular part of the organisation. It could be the size of the audit fee or the size of fees paid to professional advisers.

Big does not always mean best. One client of ours has calculated that its most profitable clients tend to be organisations which turn over between £15 and £30 million. The key is to find the size which is most attractive to you.

A track record in using the types of advice which we provide.

Whilst taking part of an incumbent adviser's work may be difficult, it is not as difficult as persuading an organisation to use expertise it has not used previously. We must remember that we could be the 23rd person to approach this prospect. If the prospect turned down 22 approaches previously, why will we be successful?

The image of the prospect.

Will this prospect, in the fullness of time, reflect well on us when it appears on our client list?

Potential conflict of interest with existing clients.

The potential other side of the 'Market Expertise' coin is the consideration of conflict of interest. This can be managed in most situations, but where a condition of our doing work with one client is that we will not work with any of their immediate competitors, then we must be very careful as to whom we choose as our Defined Prospects. In this situation 'conflict of interest' could become a default filter.

Triggers without Filters and Filters without Triggers

We could select our Defined Prospects purely on the basis of the likelihood of Triggers impacting upon their organisations and with no regard to the Filter factors. However, we may find ourselves with a list of Defined Prospects where there is work to be had but it may be with organisations with whom we would prefer not to deal or with organisations where we have little hope of winning the work on offer.

If we purely select our Defined Prospects on the basis of them passing certain Filter criteria (in our experience this is the implicit way this 'process' is most often carried out) then we may end up with a list of Defined Prospects who look very interesting and who may be approachable – but who do not have any requirement for our services.

The participant in the case study opposite realised that his first approach to a prospective client would not always coincide with a window of opportunity. Obvious as this conclusion is, we have often come across names of prospects consigned to the 'dump' list because they were not astute enough to buy the services offered them on the one occasion there was a face-to-face meeting.

Triggers and Filters – a Case Study

In a seminar we were running on the subject of using Trigger and Filter criteria for the selection of Defined Prospects, one of the participants who had a reputation as quite a good new business developer, let out a loud groan and exclaimed, 'Now, I see!' Asked exactly what it was he now saw, this individual related the following story.

The previous week he had had a meeting with the largest prospective client in his area. He had been trying to engineer such a meeting for over eighteen months. He planned and prepared for the meeting in some depth. He spent an hour and a half with the Financial Director of this business and felt that he had come away with nothing. He said that he felt frustrated and angry at himself – he felt that he had let himself down, though he could not identify what he had 'done wrong'.

Then in our workshop he realised the problem. In his own words, 'There just weren't any Triggers of any significance impacting on their business at that point in time. They had no reason to change anything they were currently doing.' When asked what he planned to do next he came back with the right answer. 'I'm going to keep in contact with them until a Trigger does happen.'

USING TRIGGER AND FILTER SELECTION CRITERIA

To use triggers and filters we need to go through the following process:

1. *Agree on the main Trigger and Filter criteria with which we wish to screen our prospects.*

   We should select between six and ten factors in total. Filter factors should not heavily outweigh Trigger factors. If we choose fewer than six criteria we will not get a balanced enough view of the 'value' of the prospect. If we choose more than ten criteria we are likely to make the process over-complicated and use up too much time carrying out initial research.

2. *Set some form of measurement or scoring on these Trigger and Filter criteria.*

3. *Decide the minimum criteria or score for a prospect to qualify as a Defined Prospect.*

4. *Screen out possible prospects using the Triggers and Filters Selection Criteria.*

   This will probably involve some research, as our own general knowledge will rarely be enough on which to make decisions as to where a prospective client scores – particularly in respect of some Trigger criteria.

The outcome of the exercise should be that the basket of prospects which we screen initially will fall into three categories. These categories are:

1. Organisations considered to be unsuitable as future clients.

2. Organisations which should be treated as Key Defined Prospects and receive the personal attention of someone (or a team) involved in new business development.

3. Organisations which fall between these two extremes. With these organisations we should focus our more broad-brush marketing efforts. Whilst we would not want to devote a lot of personal professional time to pursuing these types of prospects, if they received our regular bulletin and later asked to talk to us about a particular issue which they were facing, we would certainly not turn them away.

Figure 2.1:   Applying Triggers and Filters selection criteria – an example

Triggers and Filters Selection Criteria	Value		
	0	**2**	**5**
New regulation or legislation	Little or none.	Some – having some impact – but not likely to be severe.	Serious impact upon prospect. Likely to happen in near future.
Market changes	Some – but not sudden or likely to have serious impact.	Future fluctuations likely to be more severe.	Market subject to certain severe changes in future.
Incumbent competitor changes	No change in incumbent's offering or management.	Some change in incumbent's policy toward clients.	New client partner appointed or major change in client service.
Prospect growth	Changes in size imperceptible.	Growing steadily.	Fast growing and likely to continue so.
Our 'story to tell'	No track record in their industry.	Some successful work in their industry.	A very strong understanding of their industry.
Introductory services	We know of none.	We may have connections we can use.	We definitely know people who can introduce us.
Image	Probity could be an issue.	Moderate but not a powerful positive image.	Potentially a 'name' client.
Size	Employs fewer than 200 people.	Employs between 200 and 500 people.	Employs more than 500 people.

RESEARCHING FOR TRIGGERS AND FILTERS MATCH

So how do we carry out the fourth step of screening prospects using Triggers and Filters selection criteria?

People tell us regularly that it is not difficult to assess a match against the Filter criteria. We can quickly find out if someone knows someone within the prospect, we know if they are in a business where we have a story to tell, it is not difficult to get a picture of how big the organisation is, etc. This is probably why, when professionals use any sort of selection criteria for prospects, these selection criteria are almost always some form(s) of Filters. They are easy to assess.

How do we find out about some of the Triggers? How do we find if a company is planning a major diversion from what it has done in the past? How do we know if a business is badly positioned to deal with a new initiative in the marketplace? How do we know if the financial director has suddenly left?

This is where having some market focus and specialisation makes the process a lot easier. If a professional is market focused, he will hear a lot of intelligence in his day-to-day work. This is helpful but does not qualify as 'research'.

By subscribing to the main journals read by the market sector on which he is most focused, a professional can quickly learn of the issues which are impacting on players in the market, he can ascertain who is doing well and who is threatened, he can learn about who is expanding and who is entering new market arenas and he will learn of the movements of senior people. This type of information is the basis of trade journal journalism.

The sources of information which will give intelligence on potential Triggers impacting on possible prospects can be:

*   *On-line and CD ROM databases.*
    There are a number of extensive databases which are available in electronic format. The cost of using these databases is calculated based on a combination of subscription and/or usage charges.

*   *The Internet.*
    New databases are being made available on a regular basis via the Internet. Charges for this data are based upon the amount of information extracted.

    In addition, a fast-growing number of organisations have web sites which contain a lot of useful information for the researcher. We know of individuals who, when looking for information on potential prospects, make the Internet their first port of call.

*   *Analyst research.*
    Analyst research is produced on industry sectors and on major players within industry sectors. The information and projections can be quite detailed.

*   *Company search information* – available from Companies House.

- *Financial searches carried out by commercial organisations such as Dun & Bradstreet.*
  One should always bear in mind that this information will be historical. It can be very useful in building a picture of a prospect and its progress in recent years but there can be a big gap between the last year end results reported and the position today.

- *Trade newspapers and journals.*

- *Latest report and accounts and other brochures and material available from the prospect.*
  We continue to be surprised by professionals who see a problem in finding data on Triggers but have not picked up the telephone to ask for an up-to-date brochure on their prospect.

  The opportunity to walk into the reception of a potential Defined Prospect should not be passed by either. Reception areas very often have copies of the latest brochures, copies of the company newsletter or newspaper and a book full of clippings about the organisation.

- *Clippings services.*
  If we have an interest in a company, we can subscribe to a clippings service which will pass us all press material generated on that organisation.

- *Local business press.*
  Most towns or areas where businesses are prevalent will have a local business newspaper or journal.

- *Chambers of Commerce or Business Links.*
  Without doubt there is more published information on large organisations. Information on small or even medium-sized local businesses is not likely to appear on an international database. However, if we are seeking to develop work with smaller types of business it is worth speaking to the local Chamber or Business Link.

  In addition to the information they may provide, it is possible that these connections, if cultivated carefully, could provide referrals and introductions.

The effort involved

This sounds like work. It is. To build the right Pipeline we have to put in the accumulated efforts and activities. This includes the efforts to research and define those prospects we wish to populate the P1 segment of the Pipeline. The effort has a pay-off – we avoid the potential GIGO scenario.

Also, as someone once said, the greatest opportunities in life usually come disguised as hard work.

DEFINED PROSPECTS AS CLIENTS

Working with one of our clients recently we knew we were making headway when one of the senior people in the organisation stood up in front of his people and said:

> 'We have two sorts of client. There are those that we do business with today and there are those that we do not do business with today, but we will do business with in the future. We treat both types of client the same way.'

This attitude is in stark contrast to common practice. It is common practice that clients receive lots of attention. Clients get entertained. Clients are called on a regular basis.

It is also common practice that prospects get a telephone call once every blue moon if business looks desperate.

Our client who made the statement above had taken his people to a point where developing on-going relationships with key prospects was very much part of the day-to-day activities of the professionals within his business.

An indication of how far down this path a firm has progressed can be assessed by asking those people who have the responsibility for new business development to show the records and files they keep on their existing clients, then show the corresponding records and files on the prospects for whom they are responsible. Is there any comparison?

When people move in a firm or when they leave, it is common practice for their clients to be handed over to other professionals. This handover involves the physical transfer of material. How much handover of P1, P2 or even P3 Defined Prospects occurs? The experience of professionals to whom we have addressed this question is abysmal. Usually the answer is 'Nothing'. Either these assets have never been developed or they have been discarded.

Professional services firms serious about developing new business must develop the mentality and processes to ensure that Defined Prospects are treated like clients.

Chapter 3 **Marketing the Firm**

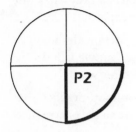

Introduction and the 'Nearness to Client' Pyramid
Corporate Marketing
Capability Marketing
Contact Marketing

INTRODUCTION

Philip Kotler, the marketing guru, defines marketing as 'a social and managerial process by which individuals and groups obtain what they need and want through creating and exchanging products and value with others'. As a description of the marketing process undertaken by professional firms this definition lacks one vital element – the importance of developing and then sustaining excellent relationships.

Nowadays the general understanding of marketing within most professional firms is high but the amount of activity actually undertaken by professional staff to implement marketing initiatives is usually quite low. We have seen much enthusiasm towards active marketing as a concept but the reality often is that passive marketing is relied upon to generate new clients. If professional firms are to win new clients, they will have to adopt a different approach.

The marketing of professional service firms should be focused on generating enough motivation in selected potential clients for them to want our services. The latter parts of this process have to involve face-to-face contacts which ultimately produce discussions ending in positive decisions. Professionals find a variety of terms to describe the later stages of this process – few of which normally mention 'selling'.

In his article 'Teaching Smart People How to Learn', noted writer Chris Argyris concludes that because professionals are experts, they rarely experience failure and over time they become quite risk averse. However, selling is a 'numbers game' where there is always a level of 'failure'. As failure is culturally unacceptable among professional people, they find ways of avoiding it. Marketing and selling therefore become low-level activities, or ones where reasons for any failure have to be made acceptable to the firm and colleagues. This often produces a distorted picture of the marketplace.

Therefore the primary aim for all professional service firms' marketing should be to 'motivate Defined Prospects to *want* to meet with us'. This aim will help to lessen the natural feelings of professionals that they are 'forcing themselves upon a prospect'!

In this chapter we will examine where passive and active marketing should be used – ensuring that all marketing activities are fully linked into a series of events and that follow-up actions happen. These actions will accumulate and help to build the trusting relationship which is necessary before a prospect will commit to becoming a client.

Professional service firms marketing can be split into three main areas, as illustrated in Figure 3.1, the 'Nearness to Client' Pyramid.

• *Corporate marketing activities:* these activities build the image of the firm and create a general awareness of what we do.

• *Capability marketing activities:* these activities illustrate the capabilities of the firm.

• *Contact marketing activities:* these activities demonstrate the added value that the firm can provide and show how it differentiates itself from the competition. These are the activities which most powerfully build the relationship between firm and prospect.

Figure 3.1:   The 'Nearness to Client' Pyramid

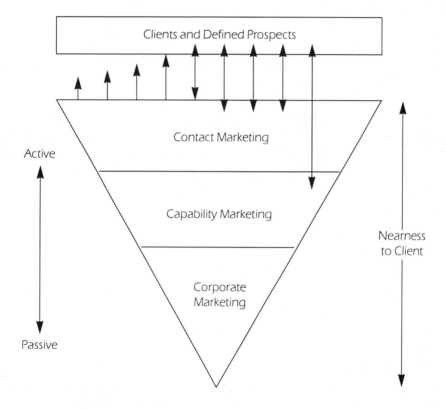

Corporate marketing

Many professional firms aiming to promote themselves feel this can be most effectively accomplished by stressing their technical excellence, size, reputation and distinguished history.

However, this rarely helps in marketing terms as:

• Competitor firms are stressing the same elements.

• Potential clients consider these elements to be the 'norm'.

Certain levels of corporate marketing are essential to ensure that people are aware of the firm and what it does. However, once this level of recognition is achieved, a much more personal level of activity is required by the firm if it is to differentiate itself and its levels of service from that of its competitors.

Corporate marketing tools and activities

Stationery, corporate brochures and direct mail

Using the corporate image consistently is an essential part of corporate marketing, therefore all printed material has to be consistent. Typography, logo design, colour, layout and any slogans must fully support the corporate image and message. Ideally these elements should generate a picture in the prospect's mind identical to the one which the firm is trying to create.

This is particularly important when promoting services which are largely intangible and has become even more critical with the introduction of new media such as video brochures and home pages on the Internet. All of these must portray and reinforce the values and messages which the firm is trying to project.

Direct mail must be used in a manner that is not unwelcome as often this will be the first physical contact the prospect will have with the firm. In this context direct mail should be linked with some other initiative such as the promotion of an event. Trying to use direct mail to differentiate a professional service firm is extremely difficult, if not impossible. 'Junk mail' has come in for a great deal of criticism in recent years. Even specifically designed direct mail must be seen by the recipient as having some 'added value' or it is likely to create a negative image.

• •

We recently spoke with a lead partner in a professional services firm who had sent out letters to 100 'prospects' asking them to fill in a quite detailed questionnaire. The benefit of doing so for these prospects was very difficult to perceive.

The Partner complained that he had only received two replies, both of which were extremely negative. Asked why he had chosen this approach to contact these prospects he replied that he believed it was the easiest method to use when everyone was so busy.

When we discussed how he felt when 'Reader's Digest' ask him to read pages of material and complete a form to win a 'wonderful prize' he agreed that this was perhaps not the best way to start a positive relationship!

• •

Advertising

Advertising is often seen by professionals as an easy way of gaining business but when this assumption is examined in detail they find that little or no business has come directly from advertising. Advertising in many professional services firms is still misunderstood.

Advertising has a role to play in developing the corporate image but often it is not analysed in terms of how many *potential* clients actually see the advertisement and, more importantly, what they can recall of the advertisement and its message. Good advertising has many positive contributions to make but fundamentally it is passive and therefore should not be relied upon to generate business directly.

Public relations

There are two forms of PR – corporate PR and specific PR. It can therefore fall into two areas within the 'Nearness to Client' Pyramid.

Corporate PR is obviously in the Corporate Marketing sector. PR generated around products or services is more specific and is a form of Capability Marketing.

PR is all about getting the firm's name known and outlining the products and services that we provide in as favourable a manner as possible. This is done via:

- TV, radio and press interviews.

- Articles written about the firm (or even written by the firm). Usually these are free.

- Advertorials. In recent times the advertorial has become increasingly popular. Advertorials are really advertisements that pretend to have editorial content – the theory being that if we make an advert look like an editorial feature it will be more widely read.

Firms that get better than average press coverage (both in terms of quantity and positive comment) appear to gain a clear advantage over those who do not. Developing good relationships with the press in our defined target market sectors is a worthwhile marketing activity. Converting PR activity from Capability Marketing into Contact Marketing can make this marketing tool extremely rewarding in terms of the time and effort involved. We will look at how this can be achieved in the section on Contact Marketing.

Sponsorship

Sponsorship of sporting or cultural events is often seen as a good 'ethical' way of raising the profile of the firm without getting too involved in active marketing. However, high-profile events cost a great deal of money and if not developed into Contact Marketing opportunities they can have a marginal contribution to the overall effort. Even lower-key sponsorship activities can be fruitful if they are combined as part of the overall marketing campaign. All of the following questions need to be addressed:

- Will this particular sponsorship opportunity have any appeal in one or more of our defined target areas?

- What other marketing initiatives can be combined with this sponsorship event to enhance and multiply its effect?

- How can we use this sponsorship event to progress any possible relationship with a Defined Prospect to a higher level in the 'Nearness to Client' Pyramid?

- Can we 'test' the appeal of the event with possible invitees before we commit ourselves?

- Can we justify the expenditure when we consider the likely success rate?

• •

The 'success' of a recent event sponsored by a major professional services firm highlighted how easy it is to allow this type of activity to run away with the marketing budget.

This one-off event was grossly undersubscribed as it clashed with another sporting event (which obviously had greater appeal to the Defined Prospects). Eventually more than 85 per cent of the firm's hospitality was taken by its own partners.

When asked how the event was chosen there was a long pause and some embarrassed shuffling before the organising partner confessed it was his own favourite interest area!

• •

CAPABILITY MARKETING

Capability Marketing is where professional services firms tell potential clients what they do, demonstrate their professionalism and more importantly start to show how they differ from their competitors. Many of the activities considered under Corporate Marketing are used in parallel with Capability Marketing activities to reinforce what has already been achieved and to show consistency.

Capability Marketing tools and activities

Product/service brochures

Specific product/service brochures can be an important part of the marketing activities as they have many uses. However, many professional service firms rely upon them as *the* central part of their marketing effort. These tools are passive and therefore are just a part of the process of moving any prospective client up the 'Nearness to Client' Pyramid toward the Contact Marketing stage.

Brochures can be used in many ways:

- They can be used as part of a specific direct mailing campaign.

- They can be used as an initial response to a request for information.

- They can be distributed at events such as conferences and seminars.

- They can be used as a 'follow-up' aid after an initial contact.

As there are many uses, we should consider design and content carefully.

- Any printed material should always have the look of a quality document which reflects the standing of the firm. There is no such thing as a 'cheap' brochure.

- The words and approach should always reflect the culture and values of the firm – first impressions are extremely important.

- Brochures should be easy to read and designed to raise the interest levels of the reader to the point where a meeting would be a next logical step. (We should not include 'everything' in a brochure as that negates the need to meet and discuss the content further.)

- The more specific the brochure in terms of target markets, the more appeal it will have to our Defined Prospects and the more it will demonstrate our expertise in that market or sector.

Public speaking events

Building the image of the firm can be accelerated if good presenters find opportunities to speak at conferences and events where Defined Prospects will be attending. This means speaking at 'industry specific' events in the firm's target market, *not* at events run in the firm's own profession at which the audience is likely to contain more competitors than prospects.

As highlighted in Section 2, Chapter 2, a well-defined speaking opportunity can demonstrate our understanding of our prospects' market sector or industry. It can also act as an opportunity to demonstrate the application of our own expertise to our Defined Prospects. Despite this, we have often heard these speaking opportunities described as a 'waste of time'. This is usually because the speaking activity has not been progressed further up the 'Nearness to Client' Pyramid and into Contact Marketing.

Any presentation must be professionally constructed and completely tailored to suit the audience and conference. A lawyer speaking about litigation *per se* is much less interesting than one speaking on litigation in the retail environment to an audience of retailers. The impression given is that this person 'understands our particular issues' and ultimately that this person or firm are seen to be 'industry insiders'. This is a large step up the 'Nearness to Client' Pyramid.

As a marketing exercise it is also critical to success that the presenter has excellent presentation skills, even if he is not the 'ultimate expert'. Often firms allow an expert to present his pet subject without considering the person's communication and presentation skills. Many firms who successfully use conference speaking as part of their marketing efforts use a team approach. A presenter undertakes the actual presentation with the expert attending to answer specific questions.

At any speaking opportunity it is essential for the firm to seek ways to develop Contact Marketing opportunities. There are a number of ways we can move the attendees to a higher level in the 'Nearness to Client' Pyramid.

- Ask the organisers for a list of names and contact details for those invited and then plan to send them additional material relating to our presentation after the event.

- If the numbers are manageable, at the end of our presentation we can tell the delegates that if they give their business cards to us – or an assistant – we will forward additional information. (This is an excellent way of establishing contact only with those attendees who have a genuine interest. This also reduces the cost of sending additional material to everyone.)

- At some conferences it is possible to hire a hospitality room for an evening. At the end of our presentation we can tell the attendees that we have this facility and invite anyone wishing to discuss the presentation further, to join us for a light buffet at the end of the day.

Conference speaking opportunities are excellent Capability Marketing opportunities if done well. However, with a little additional effort their value can be greatly increased by converting them into early Contact Marketing activities.

Newsletters

Many professional service firms have, and use, newsletters as a method of promoting themselves and their services. It is a subtle form of advertising which if done well can be a strong part of the marketing effort.

However most newsletters today appear very similar and therefore do little to differentiate the particular firm from its competitors. Most clients and potential clients are extremely busy and therefore need to be motivated to make time to read any newsletter. Therefore it is essential that any newsletter is:

- Different and attractive.

- Relevant to the reader.

- Bringing value to the recipient for the time spent reading.

Any newsletter that is seen to be 'worthwhile' by the recipient adds considerably to the reputation and standing of the originating firm.

The Internet and a WWW site

With the growing acceptance of the Internet and the World Wide Web, many firms have created their own site. There are a number of uses and benefits of the Internet for professional services firms.

- A properly designed and maintained Web page or pages can act as an additional marketing tool for the firm.

- We can use the Web site to develop and improve our image via a new medium.

- We can advertise our products or services.

- We can sell subscription products or services.

- We can offer information and/or advice in a limited format.

- The Internet and WWW can be used as a source of market research data.

- It can provide another communication channel for the firm's clients.

Successful business Web sites have some characteristics in common:

- *Successful sites are information-rich.*
  A successful site offers good content, more than a visitor can absorb in one visit.

- *The site has true 'added value'.*
  Services, content, products or other resources are in evidence. A successful site

should not just be a place to try to market and sell. Users must get real information and feel that the visit has been worthwhile through the 'added value' they have gained.

- *The Web site is a marketing channel integrated with other channels.*
  The Web and the Internet must be fully integrated with printed media as well as any other marketing activities. They are a part of the whole marketing effort.

One advantage that a Web site offers is that it can be a valuable source of information regarding visitors. Information about users can be routinely gathered through newsletters, surveys and feedback via e-mail. We are able to find out who is visiting the site and their preferences and/or reactions.

CONTACT MARKETING

Contact Marketing is where we try to demonstrate the 'added value' that our firm can provide and how we differentiate ourselves from the competition. This is where effort is put into developing the necessary 'trusting' relationship required before a prospect will convert into a client.

The process of building trust to the level required to commit to undertaking the first assignment will not usually be achieved quickly unless the target prospect has a 'burning' problem that must be resolved. Therefore, like all relationship building, enough time must be allowed for the courtship to develop and mature. During this period there are a number of activities which will further strengthen the relationship and raise the desire on the part of the Defined Prospect to want to meet for an initial business discussion.

Some of the activities below could be classed as Capability Marketing depending on the type and level of *planned* follow-up. As you will recall from the Introduction, our objective throughout the whole process of marketing is to 'motivate the Defined Prospects to *want* to meet with us'. This is achieved by a series of planned activities which link together and add value, not through unplanned and unco-ordinated actions. At an individual, practice area or firm-wide level, marketing activities are wasted if they are *ad hoc* and done 'when time allows'. Marketing achieves a high return when it becomes a 'campaign' which includes the sustained input of the right actions in the right balance.

Contact Marketing tools and activities

Articles

Writing articles is often a genuine effort to raise the profile of a professional firm. The real usefulness of any article is based upon a number of factors:

- How well the article is written.
- How relevant it is to the *specific* audience. The article must relate to the target market.
- How well the article is used *after* publication.

Not all 'experts' in professional services firms are necessarily good writers or have the natural discipline to undertake the work required to get into print. However, if a professional has a valuable idea worthy of publication the use of a journalist ghost-writer is often worthwhile. This investment can be particularly justified if the article's value can be multiplied by its usage *after* publication.

General articles about a subject in which the professional has real expertise are often lost because the reader cannot make the connection between the general nature of the content and the specific issues in her particular industry or company. It is vital that articles are written not to demonstrate the professional's specific expertise but to demonstrate clearly, in the terminology of the industry, his understanding and application of that expertise.

Most business people today have to undertake huge amounts of background reading to keep abreast of changes within their industry. Even the best articles have a high probability of not being read. Therefore the professional has to find ways of increasing the chances of an article being read by Defined Prospects.

One way of doing this is through article reprints. Most publishers will agree to reprint articles for subsequent distribution by the writer. A high quality reprint sent to specific prospects has a much higher chance of being read as it demonstrates that the prospect's problems have been identified and addressed specifically by the writer of the article. Reprints can also be used as handouts at seminars and conferences where the recognition that they have been produced by a respected journal carries more credibility than similar information published in the form of a brochure.

Research

Many professional firms generate considerable amounts of research which is of high quality and has *real* value, but it is rarely used as the productive marketing tool that it can and should be. Proprietary research is one real way of differentiating the professional services firm from its competitors. If the research demonstrates a real understanding and interest in a specific target market, potential clients will often take the initiative of seeking a meeting to develop the findings further. However, it is important that if proprietary research is distributed to potential clients then it *must* be followed up to establish if it had any real value to the recipient.

Again this is a conversational opportunity to move what could be classified as a Capability Marketing activity into Contact Marketing. The same process can be adopted by distributing research from other sources that would be of interest to Defined Prospects. Obviously the capability element is reduced as the information is not produced by the firm. However, it can still be an excellent relationship development tool.

Seminars

Seminars are favoured by many professional firms because they provide an opportunity to focus on issues which are of particular relevance to clients and prospects and to simultaneously demonstrate their authority, knowledge and expertise. Face-to-face contact with existing or potential clients in a focused environment can be extremely effective in building and reinforcing relationships. It is this face-to-face element which makes these types of events appropriate and productive business development tools.

Consequently, thousands of these types of event are held throughout the country every week. All involve a considerable investment in time and money for the organisers. Although some are excellent and productive, many fail to achieve their potential because they are not truly recognised as a marketing exercise and therefore lack the discipline that a formal marketing approach imposes. No matter how interesting and pertinent the seminar may be, without clear marketing objectives and procedures, important opportunities will almost certainly be missed.

Once the marketing objectives have been set and agreed, the 'product' (that is to say the seminar content) must be specifically designed to address the needs and interests of the target audience whilst at the same time delivering the host's desired message.

Seminars and events must not be thinly disguised sales pitches. However, the overall packaging, including style, content and execution must reflect the host firm's image and reputation. Such marketing activities should be created, planned and organised to take those attending further down the path of wanting a meeting with the firm. Therefore the organisation and follow-up of any seminar or event must be clearly planned and executed. Below are some guidelines to help turn a Capability Marketing seminar into a real Contact Marketing opportunity.

Organisation

- All letters/invitations should reflect the firm's marketing image and reinforce the underlying 'message' without overselling the event. Invitations should state clearly that they are 'not transferable' to help maintain the quality of guests.

- Based on the responses, start to allocate guests to professional staff. Obviously professionals will wish to look after their own clients and other guests whom they have invited. However, to host any group effectively there should be a maximum of five guests per person. The ratio should be less when we have 'important' guests with whom we wish to spend more time.

- Name badges should be big enough to accommodate the guest's first name and surname in a large print size clearly legible from a distance.

On the day – before the event

- Allocate each host their clients and target prospects for the event and code badges accordingly to make identification easier.

- Hosts need to be allocated a 'station', where they will stand in the arrival area. This makes it easier for the receptionists to find them. At any breaks hosts should return to their stations, as natural herd instincts will mean that many, if not all, of the guests will return to this point. This gives the guests a further opportunity to discuss the seminar or any issues it has raised in an informal manner.

On the day – the event itself

Do not give too much information away at the event. Often professional firms give away considerable amounts of intellectual property unnecessarily at seminars in an effort to impress the participants. The aim should be to provide only the minimum amount of material to ensure that the audience:

• Understands the content.

• Feels that the event was worthwhile.

• Will be motivated to ask for more.

In addition, giving away too much reduces the opportunities for making contact after the seminar and for following up any interest.

At free events try to keep something back. Then you can send it to participants afterwards. This provides another opportunity to make contact – checking that they have received the information. This allows for further dialogue which could develop a better understanding of the potential client's requirements.

If prospects show interest at the event, explain that there is more material available and arrange a meeting to deliver the material and discuss their interest further.

Feedback

Ultimately the success of any seminar must be based on the audience's judgement. Therefore getting their feedback is critical. This can be done in several ways:

• By distributing feedback forms at the end of the presentation. These are collected before the guests depart.

• By giving participants a questionnaire at the end of presentation for them to consider, complete and return later.

• By sending guests a questionnaire after the event.

All these methods have their own advantages and disadvantages, but the key point is that you must get feedback after each seminar.

Follow-up

If seminars and events are to be part of the marketing activities, they must be followed up. As marketing should be an on-going and continuous process, planning the follow-up to seminars and events is critical if their success rate (measured by the progression of the developing relationships) is to be ascertained. There are a number of ways of doing this.

• Arrange a meeting to present additional material.

• Phone the guests and ask for their opinion of the event. This can be positioned as part of an on-going drive to improve the quality of events. It can also be used as another opportunity to develop a dialogue that may produce an opportunity to arrange a meeting.

- Send all the guests a questionnaire asking for their opinions on various aspects of the event. This is particularly useful for regular events that are attended by targets who appear not to be developing to the Contact Marketing stage.

In addition, if events are held on a regular basis, they should be constantly reviewed. For example, checking the guest list often identifies the following patterns:

- The same people are invited regularly but do not respond. Therefore money is being wasted on mailings.

- The same people are invited regularly, respond positively, but do not attend. Again, money is being wasted on mailings.

- The same Defined Prospects are invited regularly, attend the event, but the dialogue does not progress any further. This is a lost opportunity.

All of these should be checked to establish if money can be saved and/or the marketing efforts be made more proactive.

Entertaining

Traditionally client entertaining has been seen as a way of saying 'Thank you' for business or for client loyalty over a period of time. However, used carefully it can also be a strong tool for professionals to use in developing their relationships with Defined Prospects. To ensure that this type of entertaining is seen as worthwhile and not misconstrued, there must be an obvious element of added value for the targeted individuals. This type of entertaining can take the following forms:

- Themed lunches.
- Discussion groups.
- Sporting/social events.

Themed lunches

Themed lunches or breakfasts which genuinely add value through either the value of their content or the quality of the other attendees can be an excellent, informal way of developing further our relationships with Defined Prospects. It is essential at these types of events that no active 'selling' of the firm is undertaken. The perception of those attending must be that we are genuinely adding value with regard to their industry, market or on a specific topic of interest. The most successful of these events have a number of common characteristics:

- The theme or topic is explored thoroughly with experts present. They may even be from outside of the firm.

- The event is not overpopulated with people from the firm. In a group of twelve perhaps there would be two managers or partners from our organisation.

- They are genuinely designed to allow free discussion and interaction rather than being dominated by the firm's representatives.

- They are planned to ensure that the opportunity for the attendees to network amongst themselves is maximised.

- The quality of entertaining is excellent but not 'over the top' – particularly in respect of alcohol.

- Timings are adhered to, with the opportunity for interested parties to continue their discussion after the formal closing of the event.

- The timing of the event reflects the needs of the attendees rather than the timing most suitable to the host firm.

- Relevant material (research, articles etc.) is available but is not seen as obtrusive.

● ●

One Consulting Engineering practice we know holds Themed Lunches once a month. These are held on a Friday at their office for groups of between twelve and fifteen people.

They try to populate the lunch with three partners and ideally six existing clients and six Defined Prospects. Sometimes they also have a guest 'expert'. Great care is taken to ensure that the relationship with the Defined Prospects is sufficiently well developed that they can see the objectives of the lunch clearly and also the benefits to them of attending.

All visitors are carefully selected so that people with common interests attend (and are seated together) but not competitors. The theme for the event is set out clearly and concisely for fifteen to twenty minutes before lunch begins. Lunch, a three-course meal with accompanying wine, is planned to take about 90 minutes. This organisation has been running these events for about three years.

Over the last year 27 per cent of the target prospects that have attended these Themed Lunches have become clients. The Managing Partner told us that he originally felt that this type of event was a poor use of partner and support staff time. However, based upon the results seen over the last twelve months, they are now fully committed to this event. Nonetheless he did stress that they see this as almost the final step in developing relationships with their Defined Prospects prior to talking about specific projects.

● ●

Discussion Groups

Discussion Groups mirror much of the above but are usually bigger in terms of the numbers attending – perhaps up to 20 or 25 people. Almost invariably the catering provision is simpler. One major benefit of discussion groups is that they are more formal in structure and therefore minutes can be taken and circulated afterwards.

Common themes and areas of interest can be identified and thereby generate further opportunities to contact the participants afterwards. This contact can utilise tools we have considered earlier such as article reprints, research outputs and conference papers.

Sporting/social events

Sporting and social events can sometimes be used as part of the process of developing a relationship with Defined Prospects but again this must be done carefully and not at too early a stage in the relationship development process.

Sporting occasions may either be events where attendees participate – such as golf days, clay pigeon shooting or go-kart racing. Alternatively the attendees may be spectators. However, not all people have an interest in sports and even those who do, may have only a narrow interest.

Social events are also likely to have specific appeal only to certain types. With both sporting and social occasions, identifying whether the particular event is of specific interest to the invitee is high priority.

Discomfort can be caused when we invite a Defined Prospect to an event in which they have no interest. Saying 'No' may cause the relationship to regress on one or both sides, sometimes unknowingly. Even worse is the situation where the Defined Prospect attends 'to be polite'. This again may cause some slippage in the relationship.

The critical issue, as already highlighted in our discussion on seminars, is to make the visitors feel welcome on arrival and throughout the event and to manage not only their attendance but also the follow-up after the event. Often because no follow-up has been considered, little – if anything – happens after the event. This can cause discomfort or uncertainty on both sides – neither knowing how to make the next move.

One final word of caution – entertaining can appear to be a rapid way of progressing a relationship; however, entertaining appeals to different people in different ways, therefore it should never be seen as a panacea.

Networking

One of the best, yet least used, marketing tools for generating new clients is proactive networking – including asking for referrals. Most professionals feel intimidated about asking existing clients to refer them to a potential client whom they may know. Yet done well, it can provide a good source of preconditioned prospects as well as making the existing client feel good in the process.

Asking an existing client for a referral must be done professionally and timing is all important. If an existing client is happy with the services of our firm a sense of pride can be generated by actually asking for a referral.

Regular contact with existing clients should focus on providing them with information and/or updates that *they* find valuable. Therefore this information should be industry- and/or marketplace-specific. Internal reports, magazine articles, conference papers and usable statistics can all be utilised. The aim is to ensure that the client believes that we are genuinely interested in not only developing the relationship but more importantly helping them develop their business or run it to its full potential.

At the end of these regular meetings, where the professional has provided information of value to the client, asking for a referral is timely and can be seen merely as a 'trade' for the value given. The execution of this activity does need to be handled well and the essential skills must be in place before any concerted effort is made towards asking existing clients for referrals.

SUMMARY

Client-focused marketing is about developing a truly proactive marketing programme for each individual Defined Prospect. Realistic and clear targets must be agreed for every stage of the process, covering both expenditure and the quantity and quality of the relevant activities. These must be monitored regularly and should include – wherever possible – 'cross-selling' targets.

Any and all target client contact must be seen as an opportunity to get the target client to *want* a meeting – not (yet) to sell. Once this objective has been achieved we can then commence the information-gathering stage which is the first part of the selling process. The following sections cover what to do next.

Chapter 4 **Making Appointments with Prospective Clients**

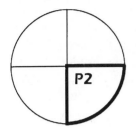

Setting up First meetings
Using a Marketing Event to Generate an
    Appointment
Making Appointments Using the Telephone

SETTING UP FIRST MEETINGS

The hope of most professionals is that marketing should create a stream of interested prospective clients who jam the switchboard with requests for meetings. This doesn't happen. However, it is not an unrealistic scenario to imagine a prospective client who is involved in a Capability Marketing or Contact Marketing event to say to a professional, 'I'm interested in speaking with you further about this, why don't we put our diaries together?' This does occur – but not enough to fulfil the new business ambitions and objectives for most of us.

Having used our marketing activity to create a level of interest, most times it is up to the professional to be proactive and suggest a way forward to the prospective client. This can happen in two main situations:

1. At a marketing event (e.g. a seminar or discussion group).

2. Via the telephone.

USING A MARKETING EVENT TO GENERATE AN APPOINTMENT

Professionals have often asked us the question:

> What do you speak to prospective clients about at a seminar – for instance at the end when you're all having a bite to eat? I feel uncomfortable in that public situation if I try to discuss their business – and I think clients do as well. On the other hand just talking about the weekend's football seems like a wasted opportunity.

The alternatives described in this question represent two extremes. The best and safest approach lies in between the two. Raising the subject of football or golf in these precious minutes is a wasted opportunity – so one must try to keep the conversation related to business. However, if we focus straight on the client's business she may feel that she is being put on the spot. An opening gambit may be a question along the lines of: 'How do you see the new legislation affecting the industry?' or 'How do you think suppliers will react to the shortfalls that are predicted?'

The sort of questions which could be seen to be intrusive in this situation could be openers such as, 'How is your company going to react to this legislation?' or 'What pressures do you think your suppliers are going to bring to bear on your company?' In a public place (sometimes with potential competitors in close proximity) people may not want to deal with these sorts of questions. By keeping our discussion openers at a more generic, industry level we are introducing a discussion in which both parties have an interest and some knowledge, the dialogue is on common ground and the client can keep the discussion at either an industry level or (if she feels comfortable) a company-specific level.

There are people who will react to the question about legislation and its effect on the industry with the sort of reply which goes something like: 'I don't know how it is going to affect others but I do know it's a major opportunity for us. We're gearing up for a major sales expansion.'

If the prospective client introduces her organisation into the discussion – as in this example – then it is OK to continue to be more specific and focus upon her particular situation.

A tip on discussion openers

A few years ago when running a promotional seminar, one of our colleagues approached a prospective client, introduced himself and was just about to speak further when the other person jumped in with: 'If you're going to ask me what I thought of the seminar please don't.' The surprised consultant replied with: 'Sure, but why not?' The prospect replied with: 'I've had umpteen of your colleagues introduce themselves to me and then ask straight away, "What did you think of the seminar?". I think I've answered that question enough times today.'

At our debriefing meeting this situation was brought up. When we compared notes, sure enough, we found that we had unconsciously cloned an approach to opening a discussion. It had definitely turned off one person. How many more had we turned off in the past? We also realised that if we started every discussion the same way the chances were that the resultant conversation was probably similar. This was clearly not an effective way to get to know about our prospective clients. We worked on creating a number of different discussion openers and each of us took 'ownership' over two of them.

From then on our debriefing sessions became infinitely more information-rich. We were all gaining different information from our seminar participants and this gave us greater insight into potential areas where we could provide assistance. Simple and obvious – in hindsight!

Suggesting the meeting and gaining commitment to the meeting

Success of a marketing event can be measured by the quantity and quality of face-to-face meetings held to discuss prospective clients' business issues. Realising this, professionals sometimes put themselves under undue pressure to get these meetings in the diary as soon as possible. The thinking is, 'Strike while the iron is hot.' In other words, if the prospect seems to show interest, put diaries together there and then.

The question is, does this approach put the prospective client under pressure? Does the prospect want to be seen getting her diary out 'in surrender' to the persistent professional who has spotted an opportunity and is 'striking while the iron is hot?' If, through the professional's eagerness, the prospective client does feel obliged to agree there and then to a follow-up meeting, the cancellation of this meeting is only a secretary's phone call away.

We do want Capability Marketing and Contact Marketing events to produce business meetings but we do not want the prospective clients feeling at all pressurised. Such a start will never lead to any sort of relationship being established.

If it appears there are grounds for a one-on-one meeting to explore problems or solutions, the professional could introduce this along the following lines:

> I believe we could help you with this opportunity but here is not really the place to discuss this further. When I get back to my office I'll drop you a line with a couple of key thoughts on what we could do, then give you a call to see if it is appropriate to meet. How does that sound?

If our marketing has done its job, if we have been professional and assertive (but not pushy and aggressive) in our approach to the prospective client and if we can formulate an effective tailored letter which precedes our telephone call (see 'Preparing the ground' on page 52) then we will gain an appointment. Moreover it will be executed in a way which is professional in approach and is going to be comfortable for the majority of people – both prospective clients and professional staff.

There will be occasions where the prospective client has seen enough and wants to explore things further by initiating a business-focused meeting. In this situation the suggestion of a letter and then a follow-up telephone call would be not only coy but wholly inappropriate! Grab the diary and agree a date and time!

MAKING APPOINTMENTS USING THE TELEPHONE

Image

When discussing new business development with professionals this is probably the most emotive topic. Hang-ups, fears, prejudices and stereotypes quickly become part of the conversation. Phrases such as 'double-glazing salesman', 'cold calling' and 'unwelcome and unexpected intrusion' are common currency.

The simple fact is that most professionals have a mental image of 'cold calling' and they do not like this image. However, most professionals have at some time tried to use the telephone to make appointments. Not all of the negative images are baseless. A lack of success in gaining appointments compounds the negative image.

Perceived problems

When we ask what, specifically, professionals have difficulty with when using the telephone to make appointments, the typical replies include:

- Getting hold of the person – busy senior people are invariably tied up with other tasks and meetings.

- How to ensure that we are not intruding on the person – after all we cannot see what is happening in her environment.

- Getting past the secretary who acts as a 'gatekeeper'.

- Knowing how to open up the telephone discussion with someone we may never have met before.

- What to say to the person to interest her in a meeting.

- How to deal with the objections and resistance which a person may have to meeting with us. How do we deal with the person who says she is working with a competitor or the person who asks us to send literature when we really want a meeting?

- How to ask for the meeting.

If we understand the principles of making effective appointment-seeking telephone calls and apply some thought, simple planning and practice, most of the above problems can be diminished considerably and some we can eliminate altogether.

Phoning for appointments – the three situations

There are three main situations in which the professional could be making a telephone call with a view to agreeing an appointment.

- *Situation 1*
  We are ringing to make some appointments following a marketing event. We have had some face-to-face discussion with the individuals concerned, although this will probably have been quite brief and in a public setting.

- *Situation 2*
  We are ringing for appointments with senior people within a prospective client. Despite our best marketing efforts we have never managed to meet them face-to-face.

- *Situation 3*
  We are ringing for an appointment following a referral from a third party to the person concerned.

When to call

Let us imagine an example based on Situation 1.

The Discussion Group met last Thursday. On Friday we sent out follow-up letters to six people with whom we (or our colleagues) had had some discussion. These letters would have arrived on Monday. In the letters we said that we would call on Wednesday. (This allows two days for the letters to be read but is not so far into the future that someone reading the letter on Monday morning is likely to have forgotten it.)

Imagine it is Tuesday evening and we are about to go home. Before we do so we think about the calls we are going to make the following day. On the (realistic) assumption that we know nothing about the prospective client's movements, *when should we make these calls?* Assume that we can dedicate an hour to this task on the Wednesday.

We have asked this question of hundreds of professionals and every permutation possible has been suggested. The most popular are 'ten o'clock to eleven o'clock' and 'lunchtime'.

Our experience and the experience of people who have measured their success in making appointments on the telephone shows clearly that these are the very worst times. People are rarely available over lunch and are unlikely to be in their offices. If we look in the diaries of senior people within organisations and examine their activities between ten and eleven we find they are mainly involved in meetings and are not available to take telephone calls.

The best hour? Use half an hour from eight thirty to nine (some will argue eight fifteen to eight forty-five). Then use half an hour from five thirty to six (alternatively five forty-five to six fifteen). The explanation is simple. Many senior people start early and/or finish late. Very often this 'overtime' is spent in their offices and they are less likely to be involved in meetings. It is usually easier to get directly through to them as well. Secretaries tend not to work the extreme hours kept by their bosses.

People have said to us that if a senior manager is in his office at eight in the morning he is using this time to carry out work free of interruptions. Our telephone call will therefore be intrusive. There are two answers to this – one serious and the other slightly tongue-in-cheek. The serious answer is that we should always check to ensure that we are not interrupting anything critical. (We show how to do this under the heading 'How to make the call' on page 53.)

The tongue-in-cheek answer is that perhaps it would be more convenient to interrupt this person in the middle of a board meeting instead. Senior managers go to work to achieve things. However, they all have a telephone on their desks. Most calls received are not anticipated. The telephone is by definition an interruption. We are simply trying to contact this person at a time when she is available to take a call and is not involved in totally uninterruptable activities.

Personal organisation

It is eight o'clock on Wednesday morning. Before getting down to making the calls it is probably a good idea to go through the morning's post. A couple of items look urgent and can be fixed quite quickly. A telephone call fixes one. A brief discussion with a colleague should sort the other. The brief discussion is not so brief. Another subject is dealt with as well. Time to hit the telephone . . . after a coffee. At the coffee machine we have a chat with people we haven't seen for a few days. Must start the calls . . . a breath of fresh air would be nice before we get under way. Then a visit to the toilet – don't want to have to stop halfway through the telephoning task. Now, back at the desk, where are the files? A note on the desk from George asks us to call him. No – let's get on with the calls.

First call. He's in a meeting. He'll be tied up all morning. Goodness, it's gone nine fifteen. Better deal with this note from George. George situation now all dealt with and time for some more calls. Next one – out for the day. It's nearly nine forty-five now. Where does the time go? By the time we have stood up and strolled about to stretch our legs it will be gone ten. Didn't that trainer say that we were wasting our time calling after ten o'clock? Better pack it in. Still, I did try – but I knew it was a pointless exercise.

You may have seen colleagues go through this exercise. Two hours in the office. Total time spent on the telephone to prospective client organisations – 53 seconds.

The first thing we need to organise is ourselves. If our first pass at contacting the prospect is to be from eight fifteen to eight forty-five we have to hit the phone for thirty minutes and ensure that all the other (welcome?) interruptions are eliminated. Try to find a location to make these calls where interruptions are less likely to occur. Tell others that we are incommunicado for half an hour. Put a sign on the door.

The Defined Prospect file

In Chapter 2 of this Section, under the heading 'Defined Prospects as clients' (page 29) we suggested that people who were serious about their new business development should have Defined Prospect files. These files fulfil a very useful purpose at the point where we are telephoning for the appointment. They should tell us all of the marketing activities we have directed toward the prospect. They should contain copies of all tailored letters and other correspondence we have sent to the prospects in question. They should include useful names and other notes which may be reference points either just before we make the call or when we are carrying out the call. Two pieces of information which should always be included in the file are:

1. *The name of the secretary of the person we are trying to contact.*
   Secretaries are usually seen as a negative block. This can become a self-fulfilling prophecy. If we see them as an obstacle to be overcome then this can reflect subtly in how we deal with them. They sense this and believe our intentions to be against the interests of their boss. They then become more protective of their employer and defensive to our approaches. Our paradigm is reinforced.

When we ring an organisation and ask to speak with a named senior manager, the receptionist puts our call through. It is rare that this will go straight through to the person we have asked for (except in the out-of-hours scenario). The most common situation is that a female voice will answer. By knowing the name of the person's secretary we can greet her with, 'Good morning, is that Jill Hearn?' The very worst we can expect to receive in reply is, 'I'm sorry, Jill's away from her desk at the moment.'

If Jill Hearn answers the telephone we have demonstrated that we recognise her as an individual – through the use of her name. We can then begin to work with her to see how we can get to speak with her boss. If we are so focused on getting through to her boss that it is clear we don't care who she is and what she's called, this 'Hey you' attitude will be sensed. We cannot expect consideration from others if they sense no consideration from us.

It is easy to obtain the secretary's name. A telephone call at any time before we seek to make the appointment will elicit this information.

2. *The gist of previous telephone contacts we have had with the person concerned.*
One of the easiest ways for a professional to put himself under pressure when trying to make appointments via the telephone is to fail to challenge the unquestioned assumption that 'You only get one bite at the cherry.' This is where telephoning for appointments for a professional services firm is totally different from the situation where the 'seller' is offering a transactional type of product or service.

It could be argued that if we were selling advertising space in a magazine and we wanted to meet with prospective clients, we could use the 'pillage, rape and burn approach'. Using this approach we call up a prospect, try to sell them the idea of a meeting and if they don't agree we toss the prospect card in the bin and get on with another call. If the telephone call has not gone well we can call the prospect a few names as the card heads toward the bin. If she has really upset us we can express our thoughts to her on the telephone. It doesn't really matter too much because there is the rest of the Yellow Pages to work on.

Professionals are not in this game. We have spent time searching for a limited number of organisations which best fit our Selection Criteria. They appear to be a close match for our Filter Factors and we believe there to be some Trigger Factors impacting upon these Defined Prospects. We have spent time, effort and money marketing our firm to these highly desirable prospects – trying to get our name recognised, trying to promote awareness of our capabilities. Surely, if one of these prospective clients says she does not want to meet us, we are not going to consign this organisation to the bin? How many more prospects are there like this one? How much effort will it take to get another prospect to this point?

We have to look at the approach to the prospect as a potentially long-term project. The proactive appointment-seeking telephone call is just another part of this process. When we ring the prospect it should be because we believe there is specific merit in us meeting. The prospect may not agree that the issue we have raised is sufficient reason for us to meet. In this case we must be courteous and leave the door open for another approach. We must always finish with the prospect having the feeling that she will at least speak with us again on the telephone.

Therefore the time in which the 'relationship' is maintained over the telephone could be quite extended. We have personal examples where the time between first telephone contact and first meeting has been eighteen months to two years. During this time there may have been six or seven telephone calls which we had initiated – all with the intent of trying to set up a meeting.

It is far easier to make the second telephone call to a Defined Prospect if we can link this call back to the first discussion we had. Early in the telephone call we may say, 'Jim, you may recall that when we spoke three months ago you told me that it would be more opportune to speak when you had your new Sales Director on board. You were hoping to appoint him last month. How has that gone . . . ?'

A basis of dialogue has been established.

There is an old expression which goes: 'A poor pencil is better than a good memory.' We must make notes on what transpires in our telephone discussions with prospective clients. In every way we should be seeking to take the word 'cold' out of the proactive appointment-seeking telephone call.

Preparing the ground

Except in 'bushfire' situations the prospective client should never receive an unexpected telephone call. One way in which we can differentiate ourselves as professionals is to ensure that the person we wish to contact is made aware that we are going to ring. This means that first we must write to the person concerned.

This approach has been challenged at times. The typical challenge is: 'If she knows you are going to ring she can tell her secretary to tell you she's not interested or even get her secretary to write back saying just that.' Our response is that this is perfectly OK. If the prospective client has considered our letter and decided that the issue we have raised is not worthy of her time and attention right now then what are we going to do if we adopt the alternative tactic of 'surprising' her with an unannounced telephone call? Will this somehow 'trick' her into giving us a meeting?

The tailored letter

The tailored letter which precedes the telephone call should make the call easier. In essence the letter should sell the reason for the meeting. Most people find it easier to consider and encapsulate their thoughts on paper than to express them instantaneously over the telephone. The tailored letter allows this.

The tailored letter should:

- *Be one page in length.*
  This includes addresses, salutations and signatures. Anything longer than one page is likely to go on the 'too difficult' pile and therefore remain unread. The one-

page discipline forces us to focus on how we express succinctly what we believe we can do to help the prospective client.

- *Not look like a mailshot.*
  The tailored letter must have the look and feel of a personalised letter to the person concerned. If it looks mass produced and has a 'cut and paste' generic message it is likely to remain unread or will be forgotten very quickly.

The letter should be formatted as follows:

1. Introduce an issue which we have reason to believe will be of interest to this specific Defined Prospect. This will usually be related to a Trigger Factor we have discovered in our research.

2. Indicate that our firm has the capability and experience to help the prospect's organisation to deal with the issue concerned and deliver benefits.

3. Suggest that the way forward is to meet.

4. State when we will call the prospect. (This gives notice to the prospective client and probably more importantly for some of us, helps to instil the discipline to make the telephone call.)

The first line should motivate the prospect to read the first paragraph. The first paragraph should motivate her to continue reading the rest of the letter. The letter itself should motivate the prospect to take our call.

Examples of tailored letters may be found on pages 54 and 55.

How to make the call

Keep it brief

The aim is to gain agreement to a meeting, not to have a telephone conversation. Also our tailored letter should have done a lot of the selling work. Therefore there is no reason to have a long telephone discussion. Successful appointment-seeking telephone calls are rarely longer than a couple of minutes.

Speak distinctly

Make it easy for the other person to listen. Whilst the odd 'um' or 'er' is not a distraction, a person who punctuates his sentences with many of these 'foghorns' becomes difficult to listen to.

Smile

All of us prefer to talk with people who are happy rather than those who appear sour. We know instantly the expression on a person's face when we hear their voice on the telephone. A smile is transmitted clearly.

Sound enthusiastic and alert

Sit up straight or even stand to make these calls. Voice projection improves and standing makes some people feel more confident.

SJ/JH

30th February 1999

Mr J Akers
Group Technical Director
Gorgon Industries plc
Caxton Road
Corby
Northants
NN14 3RD

Dear Mr Akers

Last month's launch of URA-based polycyclamides threatens the very basis of the European polypop industry. The unprecedented level of patenting around this new technology is clearly designed to give the Dabonian manufacturers an unchallengeable position in the marketplace.

These conclusions have been well aired in the press in recent weeks, they have been borne out by our own research and no doubt they have provided a major discussion point in your boardroom.

At Clirina Sciences we believe we can help. Our specialisation is in working with clients and helping them to fast-track develop new competitive products. We use advanced technology and sciences as the basis of this work. Contrary to some informed opinion we do not believe necessarily that the Dabonians will develop a five-year lead. We believe it may be possible to leapfrog this technology.

As your company has a major stake in this market we would appreciate the opportunity to meet with you, to see if the capabilities of Clirina can be utilised to help Gorgon Industries to meet this new challenge.

I will give you a call on Tuesday afternoon with a view to setting up a mutually convenient meeting.

Yours sincerely

Sandra James
Head of Technical Research

KW/JH

21st February 1997

Mr N Seaman
UK Senior Partner
JSA Partnership
Jupiter House
Churchfield Road
London
SW8 7EU

Dear Mr Seaman

To quote the Financial Times article of 23rd January and your Times advertisement of 14th February, a key element in the success of your MVC programme will be the ability of your people to generate 'a stream of ideas on how to improve financial performance' and a 'raft of ideas for improvements'.

The analytical skills of your people will be absolutely necessary in this process – but they will not be sufficient. As the Financial Times article pointed out, many of your competitors are somewhere on the same road as yourselves. A significant key to differentiating JSA Partnership will be achieved if your people have the ability to think laterally – as well as analytically. The person proficient in these two skills is much more likely to add value to the client than the person proficient in only one.

At Anstrom Business Partner a significant amount of our consultancy and training work is carried out in the Professional Services arena. We understand this market and have credibility within it. We also have the skills and accreditations to train professionals to add value to their clients' businesses by generating valuable ideas – sound, tested ideas not attainable through 'normal' analytical thinking processes.

We firmly believe that what we can bring can help to assure the completeness of the MVC concept and therefore its ultimate success.

We would appreciate the opportunity to take an initial discussion with you on this subject. I will give you a call to this end on Thursday 27th February.

Yours sincerely

Keith Williams
Senior Manager
ANSTROM BUSINESS PARTNER

Project an assertive image

When asking to be put through to the prospective client simply say, 'Freda Jones please', or add, 'It's Keith Williams here from Anstrom.' The tone of voice should suggest 'she is expecting my call'.

Too many 'foghorns' can create an image of uncertainty. The listener can interpret these as the speaker trying to create thinking time because he is not certain of his message. Avoid words like 'perhaps', 'possibly', 'hopefully', and 'maybe'. A hesitant voice, a lot of foghorns and the use of words not carrying a message of certainty hardly add up to the person most of us would like to meet with for an hour.

Be natural and reasonable

Listen to the replies we receive from the other person. Whilst we should be prepared for all the responses which may come our way, we should not be so rigid that the other person has reason to believe that our replies are programmed.

Don't get involved in a 'fight' with the prospect's secretary

There is no winning such arguments. The secretary will be doing her job – probably as instructed by her boss.

At the same time don't accept the 'I'll get her to call you back' response from the secretary. We all know from experience that these call-backs rarely happen. If they do we are usually engaged in some other activity and are not well prepared to handle the call.

Try saying something along the lines of, 'I know Mrs Johnson is very busy and rather than have her trying to track me down, it's probably best if I give her a call back. Can you tell me when would be best to grab just a minute of her time on the telephone?'

Use the other person's name

This does not suggest being over-familiar or inserting the prospect's name at the beginning of every sentence. People like to hear their own name. Use it occasionally.

Ensure the other person can take the call

We do not know what is happening in the other person's environment. Her secretary may have stepped outside for a couple of minutes and the call may have inadvertently gone directly through to the prospective client's office. She may be involved in a very important meeting. As we now have the opportunity of talking with the person whom we may have been trying to get hold of for some time, the temptation is to plough ahead and get our message across. This approach could kill any chance we have of agreeing an appointment.

Check that she is free to take the call. ('Do you have a minute to talk?') We can lose nothing through this demonstration of consideration and courtesy. If the other person replies that they cannot take the call right there and then we simply ask when it would be convenient to call back. Our experience is that when we call back at the suggested time the other person is usually quite willing to take the call. One courtesy generates another.

Know exactly what to say

Having trained hundreds of professionals in how to use the telephone to make appointments we are used to the initial feedback that professionals do not like the idea of having a script. When we explore this more deeply what people are really concerned with is 'sounding scripted'.

Professional actors do not sound scripted when they act out a scene but they are certainly not ad-libbing! They are working to a script which not only instructs them in what to say but how to say it and how to support the words with movement. Their polished performance comes with practice, committing the words to memory and developing familiarity with the message. The same is true in respect of using a telephone 'script'.

The alternative to not having worked out exactly what we want to say is to have a general feeling about the message and 'play it by ear'. Having listened to thousands of real and role play appointment-seeking telephone conversations, the planned message works best every time.

On training courses one of the most common learning points on which we receive feedback is the value of writing down exactly what the verbal message is to be. Another observation is how much better and more comfortable people become at carrying out this type of telephone call after they have practised three or four times.

Talk about results and benefits

If a prospective client is going to give up time to meet with us, she must believe there is something in it for her. In the telephone call we must refer *explicitly* to the outputs we could reasonably expect if there was a requirement which we could fulfil within this prospect organisation.

We should be using phrases such as 'cost savings', 'improved efficiency', 'shortened timescales', 'reduced risk', 'higher return on capital', 'increased business levels' and 'improved profitability'. These are the subjects which have the greatest chance of motivating someone to meet us. 'Leading edge methodologies', 'experienced professionals' and 'innovative project management techniques' may be interesting to us but are unlikely to stimulate the prospect.

Don't ask if she has read the letter

There is no point to this question. The possible answers are:

* Yes – in which case we may as well proceed with what we intended to say.

* No – she has not or has not had time – in which case we may be asked to call again when she has read the letter.

* No – she is unaware of receiving the letter – in which case we will have to re-send it and then call again.

This is a no-win question.

Recap the main point of the letter as if we were working on the assumption that the letter had been received and read and the message retained ('. . . in my letter I made the point that we had brought significant efficiency improvements to clients who, like yourselves, are multi-sited . . .').

Ask for the meeting

Having explained why we are calling and the reason why we believe it would be valuable to meet, the time is right to ask for an appointment. It does not matter how we ask for the prospective client's commitment to the meeting. We should ask in a way with which we are most comfortable. The tone of voice is as important as the words. Don't leave a long pause – hoping that the prospect will suggest having a meeting. It is more likely that the pause will encourage the other person to ask questions which will stimulate a discussion. Remember that the likelihood of success in gaining an appointment is in inverse proportion to the length of time spent talking with the prospective client.

Think through the likely objections to agreeing an appointment

Sometimes there are genuine reasons why a meeting may be inopportune. However, there are many common 'fob-offs' which some people use. Many of these we have heard time after time. When we are confronted with these we have two alternatives.

The first alternative is to start thinking of a good answer. Sometimes we succeed but mostly we do not. Long-winded rambling replies are the typical output.

The second alternative is to plan how we will respond if we receive one of the common 'fob-offs'. Below are some of the commonly expressed resistances which professionals tell us they meet and one example of how each of these could be dealt with. These are meant to be purely illustrative.

We find that any individual professional will:

*   Adopt some of these replies word for word.

*   Amend some to his own style and situation.

*   Reject some completely as they do not feel right or they appear to conflict too much with his style.

There is nothing wrong with any of these reactions. Even the third reaction is perfectly OK providing the professional then works out exactly what he would say. The only dumb way forward is to expect to be hit with an objection and not have any planned response.

'I want you to see one of my subordinates.'

Yes, I understand, Mrs Johnson, and I can see how his input will be valuable. Maybe he could participate in our meeting. However, at the initial stage there are likely to be issues of policy, which is why we need to meet with you also. Would sometime week commencing the 21st be convenient?

'Send me literature.'

We have literature and I would be pleased to send it or bring it. However, literature by its very nature tends to be general and what is required are specific answers to your specific situation – addressing your priorities. To achieve this we need to take a short initial meeting. When can we get together?

'You're wasting your time.'

I wouldn't consider my time wasted if I had been able to leave you with ideas on the subject which you found valuable and which could lead you to give consideration to our organisation in the future. Could we put a date in the diary sometime around the middle of next month?

'I'm already working with a competitor.'

I would be surprised if you were not. I believe that meeting with us would be valuable for your company. From our meeting you will be able to benchmark the advice and approach which your current advisers are giving you on this issue. Shall we say Thursday or Friday the week after next?

'We don't see the need for outside experts.'

I can understand that and until you have the opportunity of evaluating our potential services I wouldn't expect anything else. That's why I'm calling you. When could we meet?

'You're too expensive.'

Most of our work is done for long-established clients. The major reason why these clients continue to utilise our services is that they believe they get good payback on the investment which they make. They wouldn't return otherwise. A short discussion will establish if we can bring this benefit to *your* organisation. Would Tuesday the 4th be a suitable day to meet?

'I'm not interested.'

It would be unrealistic to expect you to be interested in something you haven't had the opportunity to fully investigate and if, at the end of an initial meeting, you're still not interested in the potential benefits we could bring to your organisation, then I shall certainly respect your decision. Would Wednesday afternoon suit?

'Tell me about it now.'

I wish I could; however, I need to relate our capability directly to your situation and your requirements. To do this we need to meet and discuss your current position. When can we get together?

'I'm too busy.'

I understand that you must be very busy, Mrs Johnson. In fact we often find our clients turn to us when their own resources are constrained. Perhaps we could meet to discuss how we could be of assistance to you on some of your initiatives? Would one Friday in the next month be convenient?

Be reasonable when confronted by what appear to be genuine reasons not to meet. ('I'm half way through employing a new person to take responsibility for all employee benefits. I think such a meeting would be appropriate when she is in place.')

The aim is not to bludgeon a meeting with a reluctant prospect. A begrudging acceptance to meet very often results in a cancelled appointment.

Professionals should always keep in mind that the appointment-seeking telephone call is just another step in an on-going marketing process aimed toward people within a Defined Prospect. If the appointment is not won, the rest of the marketing process has to go on. Another subject at another time may be the stimulus which motivates the prospective client to agree to meet with us.

What to say

The appointment-seeking telephone call should proceed through six stages.

1. Greeting and identification.

2. Check she can take your call.

3. Gain interest – referring to our referral source and/or tailored letter.

4. Ask for the appointment.

5. Make the appointment.

6. Confirm date and time.

For example it could go something like this.

Client	Good morning, Laura Johnson speaking.
Professional	Good morning, Mrs Johnson.
	My name is John Robinson. I'm a senior manager within Trilby Myers tax practice. I sent you some information in the last week and I also believe that my name may have been mentioned to you by Bill Williamson from your Finance department.
	Do you have a moment to spare?
Client	I'm quite busy so if you can keep it brief I would be appreciative.
Professional	Of course. You may recall in my letter I referred to our track record in helping clients with executive remuneration packages.
Client	Yes – though I can't recall the exact details you sent.
Professional	That's OK. You must receive a lot of information one way and another.
	The results of this type of work which we have carried out for other clients is usually a combination of cost savings, more attractive packages for key staff and reduced employee turnover.

Bill mentioned to me that you were considering examining this avenue and I'd like to meet with you to explore if these same benefits could extend to your organisation.

When could we meet?

Client	Well it is something which we want to look at more closely but it's not top of the priority list right now.
Professional	I understand – but I was thinking in any case of putting a meeting in the diary for five or six weeks hence. How does that suit?
Client	Yes, I could probably do that.

Section 3 **Selling – the Art of Persuasion**

Chapter 5 **Selling – the Art of Persuasion**

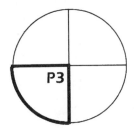

What is Selling?
Why do People Buy?
Aristotle and 'The Art of Rhetoric'
Real Needs and Perceived Needs
The Iceberg Principle
Building Trust

WHAT IS SELLING?

There are numerous definitions of selling. Many of these are constructed to support some model or framework. The model is constructed first, then the definition is squeezed to fit. We have seen some odd definitions.

We simply used the dictionary in our office to give us our definition.

The dictionary told us:

> **To sell: to persuade others to accept.**

That seemed simple enough and reasonable enough.

If that is what selling is all about, then what is the key to being successful in selling? We concluded that:

. . . .

The Key to Successful Selling

Presenting our 'case' in such a way

that it is easily acceptable to the other person

– so they find it easy to be persuaded.

. . . .

WHY DO PEOPLE BUY?

What is it that makes a customer choose one supplier and not others?

How is it that some people make a 'poor choice' when seemingly better competing offers are ignored?

As our careers in selling and business development have progressed, we have been exposed to various models and theories. Interestingly the vast majority of these models focus heavily on building selling behaviours rather than working hard to understand buying behaviours.

Over the years we have learned that:

- People buy if they buy you.

- People buy if you can fulfil their needs.

- People buy if you can lead them to the conclusion that they have needs which must be addressed and that they really are looking for a solution to these newly discovered (and now apparently mountainous) needs.

- People buy for two reasons – because they need something or because it makes them feel good.

- People buy if you can satisfy their needs *and* their wants.

We have found that none of these are incorrect – but they all fall short in some regard. This sometimes comes into focus on a training session when a participant claims that, 'I worked hard to understand every aspect of his needs, I checked it with him, I built the solution totally in line with what he said, and then he went and bought a solution with half the functionality and paid more for it. Tell me why that is.'

The trainer who is working to the model of 'needs-based selling' is struggling here. His initial thoughts are to doubt the participant's skill in understanding and fulfilling the customer's needs. However, as the trainer works with more and more salespeople, he hears the story more and more often. These salespeople can't *all* have done such a bad job. Perhaps the model of 'needs-based selling' is incomplete?

Needs and wants

A few years ago when my children were young and my job required me to carry a lot of bulky equipment around the country I looked at a 'people carrier' vehicle as a potential purchase. They were comfortable, gave good visibility, were reasonably economical, could carry a lot of equipment, were useful for transporting the family and dogs and were configurable so that weekend DIY jobs and shopping excursions could be accomplished quite easily. They were also well made, had received good reports in the motoring press and fell within my budget.

When it came time to change my car what did I buy? I think you can guess the answer. My four-wheeled solution fulfilled very few of my logical needs and I had to personally top up the budget by a few thousand pounds. So much for needs-based buying behaviour. What I needed and what I wanted were two different agendas.

Needs, wants and trust

Let us take as another example: the purchase of a pension as provision for old age. Our case will be John, a 26-year-old man, married for one year and who has just found out that he and his wife have a child on the way. They are delighted. John is not an irresponsible individual, he works but he does not have any pension provision in place.

One day John is introduced to a person who sells pensions (amongst other financial services products). This person sits down with him and runs through various

* *

A few years ago we were talking with an estate agent. We asked this person about a common complaint which people had expressed to us about estate agents in general. The complaint was about the sheets of property details which were sent out to prospective purchasers.

People who were looking for a semi-detached property in a particular area and within a certain budget were sent details of properties varying totally from this specification.

This annoyed many potential purchasers as they had to waste their time sorting through the details themselves. Surely the estate agents could put in place a simple system to resolve this service issue?

The estate agent in question agreed this could indeed be done but he would not do it. Asked why this was, he said that it was his lifetime's experience that the property that people finally bought was often a long way from what they originally said would match their needs. People who said they would only consider living on the north side of the town bought properties in the east. People who said that they needed four bedrooms and a bathroom bought a property with three bedrooms and two bathrooms.

What people said they needed and what they eventually put an offer in for could be very different. To stop sending mismatched details would simply hand purchasers to the estate agent's competitors.

* *

assumptions. When would he like to retire ideally? What would he like his lifestyle to be when he is retired? How long after retirement will he probably need to maintain this lifestyle?

The conclusion is reached that John will need to earn enough in the next 34 years to keep him in the style he is accustomed for the next 60 years! That is some conclusion. Even more startling is the calculation that he has just over 400 pay cheques (i.e. opportunities to contribute to pension provision) to come in the rest of his working life – assuming he is never out of work.

Does our 26-year-old want to live frugally for the last third of his life? No way. Does he need a pension? You bet. Does he go ahead and take out a pension? No, he doesn't.

Why?

After the pensions salesman has gone John sits down with his wife. They have a budget of sorts and they have aspirations of the things they want to do in life – some long term, mostly shorter term.

They want to take a holiday the month after next – the last they'll have before they have children. They want to redecorate in expectation of the new arrival. They want to buy a very attractive crib which they have seen in a local shop. They want to have another child within a reasonably short time of the first.

Do they need all these things – really *need* them? No – but they *want* them.

With all these priorities, the £50 or £100 per month which the pension would consume, just can't be considered right now. However, John has made a mental note that he will get some form of pension provision under way before he allows himself the luxury of a motorcycle. (Something he has always wanted since two of his closest friends went two-wheeling.)

When the salesman calls back to see John, John tells him that he and his wife have decided not to go ahead. The salesman reiterates the calculations and arguments of their last meeting. John seems to waver but holds his ground. He decides to explain in detail the things he and his wife discussed and the priorities they have. It is clear however that the salesman is not interested in these issues in John's life. He keeps interrupting with the logical arguments. It is clear he is not listening to John. In the end John finishes the meeting with, 'I understand what you're saying, but not now!'

The salesman leaves.

John is thinking, 'I understood what he said, but not now – and as far as he is concerned – not ever!' John has decided that even if the pension was far enough up his want list to go ahead, he would not buy from this person. This salesman displayed behaviours which indicated that he was more interested in selling something than understanding his potential client. Instinctively John does not trust this behaviour and people who seem to manifest this type of behaviour.

Some years on, John does conclude that the time is ripe to make pension provision for himself. He has been convinced of the need for years – now he wants to make this a priority. All he has to do is find the right person whom he feels he can trust to give him advice.

He wants to talk with someone who is very knowledgeable on the subject of pensions, someone who has a track record of advising people just like himself, someone who will listen to what he wants, someone who is not pushy; someone who will point him in the direction of the product most aligned to his situation – not their commission cheque – and preferably someone whom he can get on with. After all, there may be times in the future when his situation may change and he doesn't want to have to go through the process of finding a new adviser every time that happens.

Conclusion

Why do people buy? People buy because the product or service they decide to purchase fulfils a combination of their needs and wants and they feel they can trust the person and organisation who is supplying them.

Does this apply to every purchasing decision in life? No, it does not. The more the transactional nature of the purchase, the less the concept will apply in totality. I buy most of my clothes locally – I don't want to have to travel. Local is convenient. I do not ponder too long on where I will buy my baked beans – the cheapest will probably do. These are transactions.

However, I get my garden pond 'serviced' by a person who is neither convenient nor cheap. I tell him to do whatever he thinks is best – then bill me accordingly. Why? My experience tells me that I can trust this person totally. This is not a transactional purchasing decision. This is a relationship.

In the vast majority of instances when prospective clients are considering the use of professional advisers, they are aware that this is not a transaction. This will be a relationship – for the duration of the project or perhaps a lot longer. When we position our offering we must be able to fulfil the client's needs and meet their wants but do this in a way or through a process which enables the prospective client to trust us – to know that we are credible, capable and compatible with them.

The model as to why people buy is becoming more complete.

ARISTOTLE AND THE ART OF RHETORIC

How new is all this?

It's not. In fact it is nearly 2,500 years old.

In the early democracy of Greece, in both the Ecclesia (or Assembly) and the Council of Five Hundred, men had to justify their actions to their fellow citizens. The Assembly was also a place of deliberative rhetoric – where men urged the city to take one course of action or another. The law courts of the time could have a 'jury' of up to 500 citizens. The state did not have the monopoly on prosecutions. All who could establish a *prima-facie* case could bring their opponents to trial.

In this environment it is hardly surprising that the ability to persuade through oratory was considered to be highly important. The skill was so prized it was considered to be the second most important a man could possess. Only the skills of the warrior were considered to be more valuable.

The skills of persuasion were studied in detail, and around 330 BC Aristotle captured the essence of persuasive behaviour in writing *The Art of Rhetoric*. This writing defines the high point in Greek oratory.

Aristotle defined what it was that made people believable and persuasive; what it was that enabled some to sell their ideas better than others. He identified three key characteristics in persuasive rhetoric. In Greek these are Logos, Pathos and Ethos.

What Aristotle was saying is that to be successful in persuading others we must produce arguments which, when people hear them, are rational and logical. This is Logos.

However, this is not enough. People also respond to emotional appeals – just as people buy based not just on logic but also on emotion – what they would *like* to have, not just what they *need* to have. This is Pathos.

If the person who appeals to people's logical needs and emotional wants is also someone who is considered to have a believable and trustworthy character (this is Ethos) then this person will be successful in their attempts at persuasion.

However, all people are different and on different occasions people will be persuaded by different things. Therefore, to be successful in selling, the most effective mix of

● ●

'Of those proofs . . . there are three kinds. Some reside in the character of the speaker, some in a certain disposition of the audience and some in the speech itself, through its demonstrating or seeming to demonstrate.

Proofs from character are produced whenever the speech is given in such a way as to render the speaker worthy of credence – we more readily and sooner believe reasonable men on all matters in general and absolutely on questions where precision is impossible and two views can be maintained.

. . . Proofs from the disposition of the audience are produced whenever they are induced by the speech into an emotional state.

. . . Finally, proof is achieved by the speech, when we demonstrate either a real or an apparent persuasive aspect of each particular matter.'

Aristotle, 'The Art of Rhetoric'

● ●

emotional appeals and logical arguments has to be defined. The only person who has this information is the prospective client. The person who wishes to sell his services therefore has to define from the prospective client exactly what they would like.

We are always being told how difficult it is to prise a client away from an incumbent adviser. This is true. Even when the client goes out to tender, the incumbent is rightly considered to be in pole position to win the work next time. (This assumes that the reason for going out to tender is not dissatisfaction with the incumbent adviser.)

When we examine this behaviour in the light of the Aristotelian model it is easy to explain why. If the incumbent has been doing a half decent job for the client they will have the advantage of:

*   Being a known, and therefore trustworthy, provider.

    We often meet professionals who when told that a prospective client has decided to stick with their existing advisers, have heard the words, 'Better the devil you know than the devil you don't.'

*   Knowing the less tangible appeals which will persuade individuals in the client's organisation to support their proposal.

    By spending time with the client's people, the incumbent professional has the opportunity to be perceived as someone who is credible, competent and compatible. If he achieves this, he becomes trusted. This trust gives the professional the opportunity to get to know the *people* behind the decisions.

    He gets to know their likes and dislikes, their hopes and aspirations, their desires and their fears.

    These factors do not appear in the Invitation to Tender.

Person A in the decision-making process may want a solution which not only meets all of the organisation's rational needs but is also going to be positioned in such a way that the success of the solution's implementation will reflect upon him.

Person B may be looking at potential solutions and considering how much personal time and involvement she is going to have to commit. The more time and involvement, the worse the solution to the individual concerned.

Person C may be looking at potential providers from the point of view of personal security. If the last two projects in which this person has been involved have gone off the rails in a career-threatening way, then this will motivate him to support the safest-looking option.

All of the competing firms given the 'even playing field' of the Invitation to Tender do not have the advantage of this vital decision-influencing information. The incumbent who has used his time well has the benefit of being in a position to craft a solution which not only meets the stated needs expressed in the Invitation to Tender, but also meets the more subtle and hidden wants of important people involved in the decision-making process.

Richard Carlson in his book *Personal Selling Strategies for Consultants and Professionals* expressed this concept in the following way:

> You will never make a serious error in judgement if you expect your prospects and clients to make decisions on personal rather than organisational consequences.

We believe that Carlson may be overstating the case but we also know that there is a great deal of truth in his claim. Clients will always explain their appointment decisions in logical and rational terms but the real deciding factors may well be personal and emotional.

REAL NEEDS AND PERCEIVED NEEDS

There are times when a prospective client articulates her need quite clearly but when we explore further into the issue we begin to realise that this need is badly specified. It may simply be wrong! This often comes about when the client sees the symptoms of a problem but fails to recognise the root causes. The professional however, having dealt with these types of issues many times in the past, comes to the conclusion that there is a disparity between:

- What the person perceives as their need.
- The real need.

For example:

Client   I'm looking for help for my business producers. We're not converting enough of our proposals sent to new prospects, into work. We need help to improve our proposal writing.

The need is explicit. The prospective client has said that she needs help of some sort in producing better proposals. A few questions later the professional is convinced that whatever the quality of the proposals being produced, this is not the underlying problem. It is more fundamental. It has to do with the whole way the prospective client organisation is approaching new business development. This flawed process is being driven and endorsed by the person sitting in front of him – the same person who has wrongly identified the issue her business faces.

What does the professional do? Go along with the client's definition of the problem and produce a solution which the client is likely to buy? Tell, or lead the client to the conclusion that she is wrong and risk the person being offended or losing face – and thereby ruin the professional's chance of ever winning work from this organisation?

The right answer is to only address real needs, and deal with real issues. However, we have come across professionals who openly admit to taking on work initially addressing the client's perceived needs, then, as the project develops, changing the perception of the requirement in the client's mind.

This can work. There is a very real explicable reason why it does work. However, there are clear dangers in this approach and any professional adopting this way ahead must also be prepared for the consequences of dealing later with a disgruntled client who believes that the work was taken under false pretences.

If someone is going to tell or lead the client to the conclusion that her diagnosis is wrong, how will this person have to be positioned to be believed? Quite simply, the client is going to have to trust the professional's judgement more than her own.

Trust (Ethos) is not gained easily or quickly – it has to be earned, and mostly this takes some time. Again, the incumbent adviser with a successful track record is in a better position to challenge the client's assumptions. The new, unproven professional has to find ways of building trust before seriously challenging the assumptions and without seeming to confront the prospective client.

The dangerous tactic of taking work initially aimed at addressing perceived needs, then later changing the client's perception, can be successful because the client has the opportunity to get to know the professional. If this 'getting to know you' period is successful, then the adviser's *credibility, competence* and *compatibility* – the cornerstones of trust – are established. The professional is then in a position to persuade from this platform of trust.

However, the best course of action is for the adviser to develop trust through the process of selling. In this way the client will achieve the best solution and the professional avoids the risk of destroying trust by 'changing his story halfway through the project'.

In summary

If we can present logical arguments to most effectively answer the real needs whilst also presenting solutions which satisfy the wants – and we are perceived to be a trusted character – we are likely to have a high level of success.

To understand the client's wants and be in a position to influence the client's perception of their real needs we must have earned a position of trust. Trust is fundamental to success in selling professional services.

In brief:

* *

Perceived needs

The needs which the client thinks she has. These needs will have been reached through 'logical' thought. However, the logic may be flawed or the information base on which the logic is founded may have shortcomings.

Real needs

Real needs may be an exact replica of the perceived needs or they may be very different. A client may specify logically what she wants but when these ideas are put to the 'expert' adviser, the solution sought by the client may not serve her well.

Wants

The desires which the client would like to have fulfilled by the purchasing decision.

The wants may be parallel to the perceived needs: 'I want to be seen to be making a financially prudent decision or my credibility is on the line.'

The wants may be contradictory to the needs: 'I know we need to appoint a good agency but I want one based in town to give me the excuse to visit my friend more often.'

Trust

The state which the professional adviser reaches when he has proven to the satisfaction of the people within the prospective client organisation that he is credible, competent and compatible with them.

* *

For reasons of simplicity when, in Section 4, we examine the process of understanding the prospective client's real needs, perceived needs and wants, we will use the word 'requirements' to cover all three concepts.

THE ICEBERG PRINCIPLE

The Iceberg Principle shows these concepts in a pictorial way. The tip of the iceberg, the small part which appears above the waterline, represents people's behaviour. What lies under the waterline are the reasons for that behaviour. It is easy to observe behaviour and accept it at face value. However, if we work in any role which involves a lot of human interaction we will be more successful if we also know what *drives* the behaviour.

When we first talk with people we do not know well, people tend to express to us the things which appear factual. They focus on the tangible. They tend to speak of things which are easy to articulate and do not require deep explanation or justification. We may find in the fullness of time that appearances are deceptive. The factual may be fictitious, the logical may just be rationalisation with the benefit of hindsight.

Figure 5.1:   The Iceberg Model: behaviour and reasons for behaviour

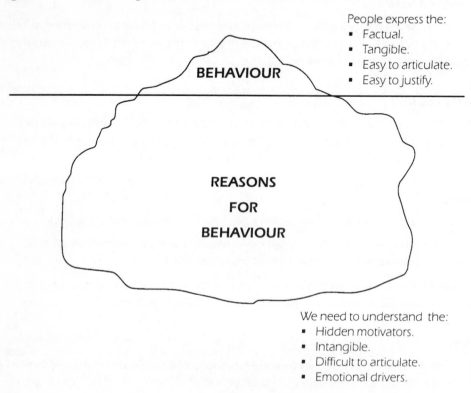

When we get to know people, we understand their 'hidden' motivators, they talk of things which are more intangible and difficult to articulate. We begin to glimpse the emotional (and sometimes irrational) drivers.

Henry Ford is credited with saying, 'People have two reasons for doing anything – the right reason and the real reason.'

In our Aristotelian model the tip of the iceberg represents the Perceived Needs – those the professional gets to learn very easily. Underneath the iceberg however are the more personal Wants. These usually take time to learn. The Real Needs we depict as a floating mass. The Real Needs may be a replica of the Perceived Needs. On the other hand they could be far removed from them.

Figure 5.2:   The Iceberg Model: perceived needs, real needs and wants

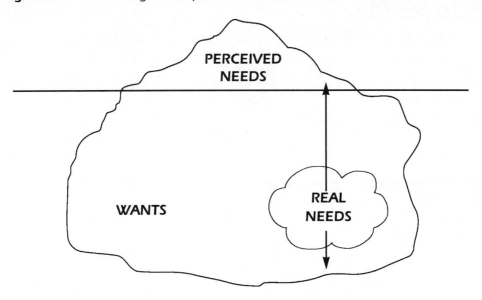

The key factor which allows us to get closer to understanding the Wants and to dealing with the Real Needs is the depth of Trust built up between the professional and the client. The deeper the Trust the better the opportunity for understanding.

Figure 5.3:   The Iceberg Model: the importance of trust

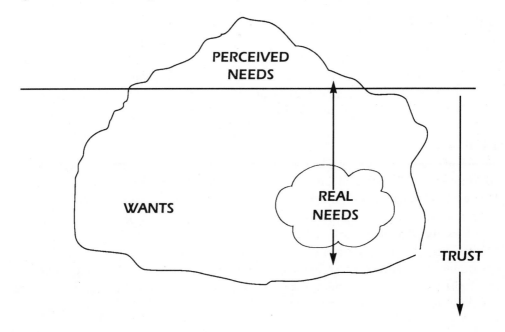

BUILDING TRUST

What you are shouts so loudly in my ears I cannot hear what you say.

(Ralph Waldo Emerson)

To earn a position of trust in the prospective client's eyes we need to build an image of credibility, competence and compatibility. To do this well and in a consistent and repeatable fashion we need to understand the types of behaviour which contribute to this positive impression. A number of these behaviours are detailed below.

Credibility

Factors influencing perceived credibility are:

Confidence

People who seem in control and confident in what they say and do are more believable than people who appear to be hesitant and uncertain. There is no one instant solution to having confidence. Real confidence comes from sustained success, and sustained success comes as a result of applying many of the factors which appear below.

It also comes from being in a situation which we recognise and where we have experience of providing valuable solutions in the past. This in turn is likely to be more pronounced if we are focusing our selling in a defined market whose issues we know well and where we have already had success. The IT Consultant described in Chapter 2 (page 22) would be, and would appear, more confident selling to a solicitor than to a high street multiple for instance.

Initial 'impact'

People are never more sensitive (even if much of it is at a sub-conscious level) than when they first meet. We 'read' the other person's behaviour and we may have indelible impressions of them even before they have taken a seat in the meeting. The behaviours involved in initial impact are observable and can be controlled and improved. We will examine these behaviours in detail in Section 4.

Honesty

A lack of total honesty may take some time to be discovered or it could be discovered the moment a few words have been uttered. In either case nothing destroys credibility more quickly than dishonest behaviour.

Delivering as promised

This is a factor influencing credibility which is not easily demonstrable early in the relationship. However, as a relationship with a prospective client develops there are multiple opportunities to deliver (or fail to deliver). Continued credibility rests on being able to deliver on an on-going basis.

Competence

Factors which affect perceived competence are:

Knowledge

Knowledge is defined in this context as the amount which we know (technically or theoretically) about a subject. Our qualifications (if recognised by a client) may give an indication of knowledge.

Track record

If the client believes that we have a record of providing valuable advice in her particular industry and type of business, this will build our competence in her eyes. Most clients do not want to act as an educator of their professional advisers – and pay for the privilege of doing so. Clients are very astute in the main in assessing if advisers have a real track record personally or whether the track record is owned by their firm.

● ●

An IT consultant who specialised in mainframe applications work was proposing for work with a client. Part of the job involved data transfer. When the term 'ATM' was raised, it was clear that the consultant thought that the reference was to 'Automated Teller Machines'. In the context of the meeting, anyone with a track record in data communications would know that the reference was to 'Asynchronous Transfer Mode'. This one faux pas was enough. The consultant did not win the work.

● ●

Expertise

Expertise is the ability to apply one's knowledge and track record to the client's particular situation and produce credible and believable ideas, ways forward and solutions. The client is picking up the message, 'I have this knowledge, I've done this before, let me tell you the best way forward for you from here.'

Searching (non-manipulative) questioning

Questions which really get the client to think in a dimension which she had never considered before, can be a real demonstration of credibility. However, this type of questioning has to be applied with great skill as there is a danger that the professional can be seen to be leading the prospective client in a pre-determined direction in which the professional has a vested interest. We will examine the whole skill of questioning in Section 4.

Compatibility

Factors influencing perceived compatibility are:

Demonstrating interest

This is achieved through spending time with the prospective client and getting to know and understand her business, the key players in the business and the issues and opportunities faced by the business. Questioning is vital in this process but there is no substitute for time invested.

Active listening

To demonstrate that we have developed a real understanding of a prospective client and the person's business, we must demonstrate that we have listened to, and absorbed, the messages which the other person has been transmitting to us. We will pay special attention to this skill in Section 4.

Adapting behaviour

'Just be yourself' is the worst piece of advice to give anyone who has the job of developing business from a wide range of people. The way we interact with a person running a wholesale vegetable business may well be different from the way we speak and behave with someone who runs a law firm. People who have difficulty in adapting their behaviour from their normal model find it more difficult to build a feeling of compatibility with a wide range of client types.

Showing we care

'I don't care how much you know until I know how much you care', could be a feeling which is common to many prospective clients.

Showing we care is a combination of many of the preceding factors. It is also about demonstrating that we are prepared to go that extra mile – or inch – for our prospective clients.

Introducing a client to a potential new customer or sending a client a copy of an article which you feel may be of interest to her are ways of saying to the client, 'I think about you and your business even when we are not doing work together.'

Showing vulnerability

People rarely warm to the 'know-all'. Professionals need to be aware of this. Professionals spend their lives being right. That is what they get paid for. However, projecting an aura of never being wrong, an aura of impersonal computer-like unchallengeable accuracy, is going too far.

Occasionally saying, 'That's my mistake' or 'I'm sorry' can have a positive effect on developing a relationship. If the prospective client comes to the conclusion that, 'He never admits he's wrong, even when he clearly is', the professional is displaying behaviour unlikely to build any compatibility.

Figure 5.4: The Iceberg Model: key elements in building trust

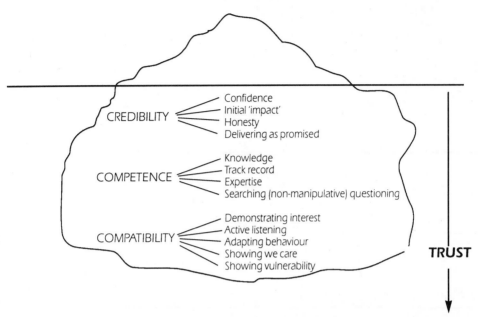

Some of the ways of building trust can be learned. They are skills or knowledge based. However some of the factors which build trust, particularly those which fall under the compatibility heading, cannot be achieved through pure technique. Technique is not enough. It is the core values of the professional and how these values map with the prospective client which can have a major impact.

Can anyone learn the techniques of selling? The answer is 'Yes'. However, the most successful people will not only have a sound application of the techniques required, they will also have the character and core values which appeal to the majority of people with whom they come into contact.

No, thank goodness, sincerity cannot be faked.

Section 4 **PACES – the Steps to Successful Selling**

Introduction to the Model

The PACES model gives a sound structure for conducting the first meeting with a prospective client. The steps in the PACES model are as follows:

P osition ourselves and our organisation.

A scertain in detail the prospective client's situation and requirements.

C onfirm to the prospect our understanding of their situation and requirements.

E xplain or explore a suitable way forward.

S eek commitment to the suggested way forward.

Chapter 6

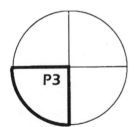

PACES: Position Ourselves and Our Organisation

BEFORE THE MEETING BEGINS

Not surprisingly, many professionals feel uncomfortable and ill-at-ease before an initial meeting with a prospective client. For many this is not common ground. Most client contact is with people we know, in many cases with people we know well. Not only are we meeting someone for the first time, we are asking the professional to carry out a job which is not day-to-day practice. This is the most difficult scenario of all – conducting a 'selling' meeting with a prospect.

The chances of 'failure' appear high. Some professionals, thinking back to previous experiences, *know* that the prospect of 'failure' is high. Unfortunately some professionals unwittingly decrease their own chances of success by engaging in behaviours which diminish their standing in the eyes of the prospective client. The development of an image of competence, credibility and compatibility begins before the visit is made and is clearly transmitted in the first couple of minutes of the face-to-face contact. The knowing professional behaves in the following way.

1. Prepare, prepare, prepare

In our training courses we continue to be surprised by professionals who openly admit to finding difficulty with initial meetings with prospective clients and tell us in the next breath about preparing in the car outside the premises or 'remaining flexible and playing it by ear'.

If we have defined the prospect as an organisation which has the makings of a potential profitable client, then we owe it to ourselves to prepare as well as we possibly can. There is more publicly available information on companies than ever before. This is obtainable in many formats, from the printed word to CD ROM to on-line databases. If we wish to display competence in front of the prospect then we ought to know something about their business. The fact that we have made the attempt to find out demonstrates a willingness to show interest.

One simple source of information is brochures and publications available from the prospective client themselves. Even quite small businesses have product information and larger companies produce all manner of publications from brochures through to company newspapers and report and accounts. Any professional who states that he is preparing for a meeting with one of the company executives is certain to be sent any information which could be relevant. Our observations indicate that this simple channel of research is often ignored.

We should use all this information to prepare:

- How we plan to open the meeting.
- What areas we aim to explore in the meeting.
- How we phrase some of the key questions we plan to ask in the meeting.

Beware! We should refrain at this stage from trying to determine what we should try to sell to the prospective client. Such an early focus can lead to myopia in the meeting and potential opportunities can be missed as the professional ploughs down a pre-determined but ultimately barren furrow.

2. Be on time

Such a guideline is so obvious – why mention it? We accept that it is a huge generalisation, but more than 60 years collective experience working in all manner of market areas convinces us that professionals are amongst the worst time managers in industry! Strange for a profession which has only time to sell.

The outcome is that lateness becomes habitual. Internal meetings never start on time, they never finish on time, people are perpetually behind the clock. The real problems start when this behaviour is visited on the client. One client of ours is a large insurance company. A new MD joined the organisation and early in his tenure he and his fellow directors were kept waiting on one occasion by one of the partners from the auditors. When he 'sounded off' about this behaviour, one of his fellow directors remarked that their auditors' people were always late and that they were forever sitting around waiting for them to show up to meetings. At this point the MD charged his people with counting every minute of management time which was wasted by the auditors. When the auditors sent their next invoice to the company for time spent working on various tasks, the new MD sent his own back in response – based on management time lost through the auditor's tardiness.

A very embarrassed and chastened senior partner finally settled the potentially explosive situation by negotiating a large reduction of the audit fee for the following year. Lateness can cost!

Some take the view that 10 or 15 minutes here or there is OK. The attitude is that after all we have to deal with the M25 and tube strikes etc. etc. Some of our clients and potential clients don't see it that way. A 10 o'clock meeting to many means a meeting that starts at 10 o'clock – not a professional who rushes into reception at 10 o'clock. If the very first impression (even before we have met) is one of a person who can't even organise himself to get to a meeting on time we should not be surprised to have our credibility questioned. At the very first opportunity to deliver as promised, we have failed.

3. Think through, and control, our 'reception routine'

How do we want to feel when we walk through the office door of the managing director of our biggest prospective client: Cool? Calm? Collected? Confident? Comfortable? In control? Not too many would disagree with these descriptions. When we are waiting in reception areas we observe the behaviour of other visitors. Many of these visitors represent companies who would like to sell their goods and services to the organisation concerned. Some of the behaviours they adopt in reception could lead to pre-meeting feelings which would be best described as flustered, uncomfortable, unconfident and out of control.

Combining a number of oft-repeated scenarios this is what we can see. The language we use in all of our examples may not be yours. However, look beyond the words and focus on the underlying messages.

* *

How not to do it

It is one minute to ten. A well-dressed, but somewhat out of breath, gentleman carrying a briefcase walks through the reception door. He is a salesman. He looks around getting his bearings. It is clear he has not visited this building before. He walks up to the reception desk where there are two receptionists. Their job is to answer the phone and divert calls to the correct extension and also to greet and sign in visitors.

Salesman   Good morning. I'm Malcolm Manning from Hermann Norris – I've got a meeting with John Jackson at 10.

His voice conveys the fact that he has been rushing to make the meeting. He sounds breathless.

Receptionist   Sorry?

Salesman   Malcolm Manning from Hermann Norris.

Receptionist   Sorry but I didn't get your name.

Salesman   I . . .

At this stage the telephone rings and the receptionist goes through her well-practised and professional routine of taking the call and ensuring it is introduced to the right person in the building. Meanwhile the salesman stands in front of the reception unit like a schoolboy in front of the headmaster's desk. He is thinking how stupid these people are. Don't they listen?! This must be the tenth time this week he's been through this rigmarole!

He has an important initial meeting with the marketing director, John Jackson, where he hopes to persuade Jackson to use his company for some promotional work in the future. He will have to be at his best as a communicator and at this stage he is having difficulty with yet another stupid receptionist who hasn't yet grasped his name. He is beginning to feel a little uncool.

The receptionist finishes diverting the call.

Receptionist   You have an appointment with Mr Jackson?

Salesman   That's right – Malcolm Manning from Hermann Norris.

The salesman looks at the receptionist. He feels unsure that she's got it right even this time. The receptionist dials an extension number.

Receptionist   Judy? I've got a Mr Norris here to see John.

At this stage the salesman leans over and corrects the receptionist hoping that the secretary on the other end of the line will hear and realise the receptionist's error. After some confusion the salesman's name is established correctly.

Receptionist   Mr Jackson's secretary says that his previous meeting is over-running. She expects he will be free in ten minutes. In the meantime please take a seat.

The salesman turns to the corner of the reception area where there are two leather seats and a sofa. Despite the fact that he has sat in his car for the last hour, driving to this meeting, the salesman feels obliged to obey the receptionist's 'instructions'. As he takes one of the capacious chairs he wonders where people buy this type of furniture. The common characteristics of reception furniture, he concludes, are that it is low to the ground, extremely soft to the point that it nearly envelopes you and consequently is almost impossible to get out of.

After a few minutes the receptionist leans over the reception unit and says:

Receptionist   Mr Jackson sends his apologies but he will be a few minutes more. Would you like a cup of coffee while you are waiting?

The salesman feels it would be rude to refuse this hospitality, and besides, he has not consumed any caffeine since he left the Little Chef 30 minutes earlier.

Salesman   Yes please, that's very kind.

Five minutes later the receptionist hands the cup of hot coffee to the salesman. He struggles to take it from her. He has to try to sit up further in order to reach the cup and saucer. Not making the task any easier is the handful of record cards which the salesman has been sorting through on his lap.

You can probably anticipate what is going to happen next.

The coffee is very hot and very good. The salesman sips it in a comfortable reverie. He then becomes aware of a presence. The presence is manifested by a pair of size 12 shoes pointing directly toward him from a distance of three feet. The salesman looks straight ahead at the suited knees of a man.

Customer   Malcolm Manning?

Salesman   Yes.

He would like to continue with words like, 'Good to meet you', but such expressions normally follow the opening handshake.

He looks up to his customer who appears to be at least nine feet tall. He feels very small in comparison. He knows he needs to get out of this chair – but how? The low table is way out of his reach. He can't put his coffee cup down. Any sudden movement and he will be wearing hot coffee. That would be a great start! He begins to move in an upward direction. His record cards fall off his lap and try to bury themselves down the side of the leather chair. He grabs at them. The coffee slops but fortunately does not spill.

The customer sees all this. He sees the discomfort of his guest and is embarrassed for him initially. It then crosses his mind that he is scheduled to share the next hour with this gauche creature. He wonders if there is any way in which he can reasonably foreshorten the meeting? Perhaps he could say that something has cropped up and could they keep the discussion to twenty minutes?

He realises that the salesman is not going to make it by himself.

Customer   Here, let me take that.

He reaches down and takes the cup and saucer from the salesman who then slides forward in the chair and pushes himself to his feet. The sitting and getting up positions have caused the salesman's tie to bulge out between his collar and the top of his waistcoat. He is also aware that his shirt tails have come out of his trousers. Does he tuck them in or does he pretend that nothing is wrong and hope that they're not showing?

Once on his feet he is confronted by a man who is a little more than average height but certainly not the nine-foot giant originally observed.

Salesman   Good to meet you Mr Jackson.

The salesman offers his hand and the two of them shake. The customer takes care. A vigorous pumping of his right hand could cause him to spill coffee over his left hand. The salesman, sensitive as ever, recognises the customer's plight. There is a tinge of red in the salesman's cheeks and ears.

The salesman turns and picks up his briefcase in one hand and a folder in the other. Both he and the customer look briefly at the coffee cup.

Customer   I'll take this for you.

The words are said out of politeness. The last thing that the customer wants is to carry this cup and saucer on the two-minute walk to his office through four sets of swinging doors.

They start walking. The salesman feels flustered, uncomfortable, unconfident and out of control. The customer wants this meeting out of the way.

● ●

Controlling our 'Reception routine'

Time spent waiting in reception should be used well and the preventable errors demonstrated by our salesman are easily avoided with a little thought. Tips when in the reception area are:

1. We should introduce ourselves by giving our *business card* to the receptionist. No one can vouch for the receptionist's hearing or memory but you can bet she can read and work out which is the company and which is our name. People with a lot of soft vowels in their name or people with unusual names who refuse to allow a receptionist to look at their business card make life very difficult for these people.

2. When signing in, have a good look at *who else has signed in* on that day or that page. If we are going to be in a competitive situation, very often the prospective client will see two or three potential providers on the one day. The reception log can tell you who they are. We know of people who turn back the pages of the reception diary, looking for interesting names. We have also seen some receptionists get very

uncomfortable with this. However, there is nothing to stop us scanning the one page in front to us.

3. Don't march up and down. This can make the receptionists uncomfortable. Move around though. There can be *a lot to see and observe in a reception area.* Some companies use it as their initial showcase because customers as well as suppliers visit. Read the certificates on the wall. What does this indicate about this company? Look at the brochures. What new information can we glean from these? Scan the press cuttings book. This will quickly indicate what activities the organisation is proud of. Read the company newspaper if there is one. What does the tone of this tell us about recent events within the organisation?

    We have often been asked the question: 'What do you talk about during that minute or two when you're walking from reception to the meeting room. You may be walking with the prospective client or it may be her secretary. The weather and car parking are rather banal. What subjects can you reasonably touch upon?'

    Our answer is a simple one. Make a point of arriving five to ten minutes before the agreed meeting time (more than this could be seen by the other person as some sort of cheap power tactic) and find something in reception which could be the basis of a short chat.

4. When it is important to be seen to be comfortable and controlled don't fall into the traps our salesman, Malcolm Manning, made for himself. Most times we do not have to wait more than 15 minutes or so. It is not too onerous to stay on our feet for this length of time. If the company is in the habit of offering coffee to guests in reception then it probably is generous enough to offer the same in meetings.

Remember, we are applying these guidelines to the early meetings with prospective clients. It is different with existing clients. We probably know the receptionist by name, she knows how we like our coffee, when we get stuck in the reception furniture we laugh about it and the client cracks a joke while helping to pull us out of the chair. Being able to make that first eye contact from a level position is simply not relevant. The relationship is already established.

But a first meeting *is* different. We have to demonstrate and earn our *credibility, competence* and *compatibility.*

AT THE MEETING

Let us take the most common scenario. We have arrived five minutes before the agreed meeting time and have checked in at reception. A couple of minutes later the secretary of the person we are to meet arrives in reception and invites us to follow her to her boss's office.

A yard from the door to her manager's office she steps aside and with a gesture indicates for us to walk into the room. In front of us is the great unknown!

This is the time when all of those dark memories can flood back. We can have visions of the most difficult person we ever met – the person who gave us a hard time from the moment we walked through the door – the person who seemed to want to personally humiliate us. We remember finishing such meetings feeling like we were a mugging victim.

Some years ago research was being carried out in New York into muggings and the victims of muggings. It appeared that there were people who lived in high crime areas who theoretically should have been subject to mugging attempts but had some kind of immunity. On the other hand there were individuals who were continual victims of muggers. Traditional groupings did not seem to explain the phenomenon. It was not a matter of size, sex or colour. As a part of the research, convicted muggers were taken to areas where muggings were known to occur. They were asked to point out people whom they would mug. Mostly they identified the same people. When asked why these people were selected, the most common feedback was: 'It's the way they move. It's something about their behaviour.'

The same applies to business meetings, in this case initial meetings between professionals and prospective clients. Usually the prospective client has the upper hand by being on home ground. They can call the shots. However, our observations totally convince us that the likelihood of being mugged in such a meeting is almost completely in the hands of the professional. If he displays the wrong behaviour and shows 'weakness' he leaves himself open to being a 'victim'.

People are never more sensitive to one another than when they meet for the first time. Consciously and subconsciously we are weighing up the other person. We all know the adage:

> You never get a second chance to make a good first impression.

It's true. If we get off to a poor start we may never recover.

If we are completely blunt, the opening of these types of meetings by professionals is weak. People tell us they feel uncertain about taking the initiative because they are on someone else's territory. They tell us they find it hard to put into words the reason they have come to see the prospective client – i.e. to sell her something. Yet in the majority of cases the professional has asked to meet with the prospect. The prospect is expecting the professional to tell her what the meeting is all about. The meeting typically wobbles to a start with little agreement to what is to be achieved or discussed.

It does not have to be this way. With some thinking and practice the professional can open this type of meeting in such a way that the prospective client is struck by an image of a person who has done this many times before, a person who is comfortable, confident and in control. The client is not made to feel they have to apologise for their guest's behaviour.

David Maister has some very telling thoughts about this phase of the meeting. From his article 'How Clients Choose' he says:

> By the fact that you are sitting here talking to me, you can assume that you have successfully marketed your firm: now the time has come to sell yourself . . .

> Your selling task is to earn my trust and confidence – with the emphasis on the word 'earn' . . .

My impressions and perceptions are created by small actions that are meaningful for their symbolism, for what they reveal. How you behave during the interview will be taken as a proxy for how you will deal with me after I retain you. Unlike the process of qualification which is predominantly rational, logical and based on facts, the selection stage is mostly intuitive, personal and based on impressions . . .

One very simple but effective guideline for opening this type of meeting with someone we have not met before, is to remember that the other person probably has three questions in her mind as the meeting gets under way. These questions are:

* Who are you?

* What is this all about and/or what is going to happen?

* How long will it take?

The professional must walk into the meeting with a very specific plan as to how he is going to answer these (usually unspoken but very real) questions.

● ●

How to open the meeting – an example

Let us take one example of how the meeting could be opened in a very positive manner – demonstrating competence and credibility.

Gestured in by the secretary, the professional walks into the office without pausing. He is carrying his briefcase and meeting notes folder in his left hand. He sees the prospective client across the other side of his office and he smiles. The client is standing, obviously expecting his entrance.

Without stopping, the professional walks confidently and unhurriedly toward the client. As he nears the client he extends his right hand.

Professional   Kate Parkinson? I'm Ray Stringer from Wright and Tyler.

He deliberately uses the prospective client's full name and he uses his full name. He wants to get onto first name terms. Calling her Mrs Parkinson would be too formal, calling her Kate would be too familiar. Transparently and respectfully he has introduced first names into the meeting at the very outset.

They shake hands. Stringer's handshake is firm but not crushing. It is dry. His plastic-bound meeting notes folder has been carried in his left hand which is clammy from the contact. He has his notes folder in his hand as he knows it will be needed from an early stage in the meeting. He has no intention of trying to find a convenient moment to dig the folder out of his briefcase when the meeting is under way.

Client   Nice to meet you Ray. Please take a seat.

She may use first names as a matter of course. We will never know. The fact is we are onto first name terms already.

The professional sits in the seat offered by the prospective client. It is opposite her desk.

Professional   Formalities first, I guess.

With this the professional takes his business card from his folder and hands it to the prospective client.

Client   Here, let me reciprocate with one of mine.

Kate Parkinson opens the top drawer of her desk, takes out a business card and hands it to Ray Stringer. Stringer takes a moment to read the card. He knows that most people think long and hard about what they put on their cards and this can say a lot about them. He looks at how the name is given on the card, he looks at the person's title, he looks for the availability of the person by glancing to see how many telephone numbers are listed.

Professional   I think I owe you an apology. I wrote to you as the Financial Director. I see
                      you are the Financial and Administration Director.

His behaviour indicates that he is observant, that he is willing to demonstrate interest and that he is open and prepared to apologise if he is wrong. It has happened in seconds. As Maister observed: 'My impressions and perceptions are created by small actions that are meaningful for their symbolism . . .'

Client   It's a very recent development. The director responsible for administration
                      retired recently and the decision was to put it all under one roof. There was
                      a lot of cross-over between the two departments in any case. It's not a
                      problem. I only got my new cards on Monday.

Professional   Good, because I was sure I had checked. Before we get under way can I
                      just check the time we have together? When we spoke on the phone we
                      talked about an hour.

Client   Could we keep it to 50 minutes? I have a meeting with the Marketing
                      Director in exactly an hour and I'd like a few minutes' preparation time.

Professional   Sure – so we need to wrap up by ten minutes to the hour? If we're in the
                      middle of something which is particularly of interest to you would it be OK
                      to finish the discussion at some other time?

Client   I'm sure we could.

The professional knows the time boundaries of the meeting. More importantly the prospective client knows that he knows and that he has noted it. She will not begin twitching and turning-off 40 minutes into the meeting, wondering how she can terminate the discussion. Subtly the professional has also indicated that he is used to working to timescales and deadlines. He knows that letting the meeting take as long as it takes is understood by many people to be pure arrogance. It assumes that the prospective client has nothing better to do than to spend her time with the professional.

Professional   Again, before we get under way, could I ask you how much you know
                      about my organisation, Wright and Tyler?

This is not a idle question. Stringer has met with people who have had all manner of conceptions and misconceptions about his firm. He knows that it is important right from the start that there are no misconceptions and that the client has a broad perspective of what his firm is about. This is an early opportunity to position his firm and to position himself. Besides, he knows that people like to know who they are talking to. The introduction of himself and his firm is basic good manners above all else.

Client	Well I do know the name. I know that you are auditors and accountants but not one of the Big 6. You sent me a brochure but to be perfectly honest I have not found time to read it.
Professional	Would it be helpful then if I gave you a short two-minute overview?

He knows it is important to get the prospective client's agreement to this. He also knows from experience that a good 'storyline' should last for one and a half to two and a half minutes. Less than a minute and a half and he won't make the best of his opportunity. More than two and a half minutes will sound long and the prospective client may start to turn off. He has chosen his words carefully. The client knows that this picture will be painted within a couple of minutes.

Client	Please.
Professional	Well, you're absolutely right that we are involved in audit and accounting work. However, our work extends well beyond these areas today. In addition to audit work we also offer professional advice in the areas of taxation (be that corporate or personal tax), corporate recovery and corporate finance where we work with our clients and financial institutions to raise business capital. In addition to this we offer specialist consultancy advice to help solve business problems in the areas of Business Strategy, Information Technology, Marketing, and Human Resources.
	We are engaged by our clients for two reasons. Firstly there may be a statutory requirement – for instance the audit. The other reason, though, is that our clients are looking to develop some form of business advantage and do not have the capabilities employed in-house. It makes sense to utilise what they need, when they need it, through us.
Client	It sounds rather like our current auditors, though we haven't availed ourselves of anything other than their audit services.
Professional	Where we do differ from other players in the marketplace is in our client focus. We specialise in working with growing businesses – businesses like yours that every now and again face new challenges which are brought about by crossing new thresholds. We really understand these issues because we work with them daily. Therefore we can offer our clients the most appropriate help and support whether that emanates from one of our 20 UK offices or one of our offices abroad.
	Statistically we lead in this arena. In the recent past we have been the Reporting Accountants for more AIM flotations than any other organisation. Does that give you a picture of who we are?
Client	Yes, thank you. I wasn't aware that you had any particular specialisation.

Professional	As for me, I am a senior manager within the local Guildford office. My particular area of expertise is corporate tax and I've worked in this field for 15 years. However, I represent the entire firm and whilst some of the challenges faced by your organisation may be outside of my own particular area, once I know what is of interest I can introduce you to the correct person – or people – from Wright and Tyler. Does that complete the picture?
Client	Yes, that has been helpful.
Professional	Good. As I said when we spoke over the phone I see this meeting as being exploratory – an opportunity for me to understand your business better, to get a feel for the issues you face in the future and to see if there are any areas where the capabilities of Wright and Tyler could be of use to you. How does that tally with your agenda?
Client	Yes, that's fine but I also have one or two questions related to a personal taxation situation. Could we find some time, perhaps toward the conclusion of the meeting to discuss that?
Professional	Shall we say we tie up anything related to the business ten minutes before we have to finish and spend the remaining time on your questions?

He realises again the value of checking the prospect's agenda. He knows it is too easy to become fixated on what he wants to achieve out of the meeting and not meet the prospect's expectations.

Client	Sure, that should be long enough. I think it is fairly straightforward.
Professional	As I said earlier, we have a wide range of capabilities. In order that we can spend as much time as possible focused on things which are interesting to you and your organisation, would it be OK to start off by my asking you a few questions? I did some research before I arrived but by definition all research is historical and doesn't tell me much about where your business is heading in the future.

The P of the PACES process is completed. The professional is now ready to move into the A and C part of the process. What is the image in the prospective client's mind? She is probably thinking:

> Here's a person who knows what he's doing. He's obviously well-practised in this. He knows where he is starting, he knows where he is finishing and he knows what goes in-between. He's planned, he's done his homework, he's structured and organised, he's observant and he listens. He is assertive but not at all aggressive. He's credible and capable and is starting to demonstrate he wants to be compatible. He has made a good initial impact.

On the other hand we could play it by ear, hope we get lucky and find something we have in common with the client.

Chapter 7 pACes: Understanding the Prospective Client

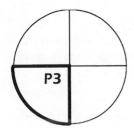

Ascertain in Detail the Prospective Client's Situation and Requirements
Confirm to the Prospect our Understanding of their Situation and Requirements

AC BEFORE ES –
A COMMONSENSE FRAMEWORK

Imagine visiting a chiropodist because the arch of your foot is causing pain. You begin to explain the problem to the chiropodist who seems to listen for a short while and then begins to take his shoes off. 'I had that sort of problem once' he says, 'and then I got these shoes. They're really great. Here, try them on. You can keep them. I've got a couple more pairs exactly the same at home.'

Dubiously you try the shoes on. They quite simply do not fit. 'I don't think these will help' you say. 'Try walking in them, give them a go' replies the chiropodist. You do. They are simply no use whatsoever. The pain in the arch is reduced due to the increased discomfort everywhere else. 'This is simply not the solution' you say. 'Think positively' replies the chiropodist. 'They positively aren't going to help' you find yourself saying.

You hand the shoes back to the chiropodist and decide to leave. As you are walking out of the door you hear the chiropodist mumbling about clients who won't listen and who don't know what's really good for them.

I guess you would not have very much faith in an 'expert' who behaved in such a way. That chiropodist would not have very many patients. Yet it is this sort of behaviour which professionals demonstrate time and time again when they are given the opportunity to engage in a selling meeting. We have observed this countless times in both real life and in role play.

Quite clearly the professional needs to fully understand the prospective client, her business, the business environment, the plans the business has for the future, how it plans to achieve its future objectives, and the risks, opportunities and issues it faces in going forward *before* coming up with services and solutions which are meant to 'help' the client organisation.

Our observations are corroborated by other notable writers in the field of selling professional services. Richard K. Carlson in his book *Personal Selling Strategies for Consultants and Professionals* states the following:

> The most common and the most damaging consultant behaviour that I have observed is the tendency to jump at any opportunity to offer a solution: When you offer a premature solution:
>
> You have a good chance of being wrong.
>
> You may not get the opportunity to come up with another solution.

So why is it that professionals so often make such a fundamental error in their selling approach? After all, the PACES model is extremely simple. It requires no great intellectual capability to understand. The 'A' of the model (ascertain) comes before the 'E' (explain). The model suggests that we ascertain the client's situation and requirements before we explore and explain a suitable way forward. First understand the problem in detail, then devise a solution. Don't try to come up with solutions before we understand the problem.

WHY PACES 'GOES WRONG'

Professionals themselves have provided the answers to us. Among the explanations we have heard are:

Explanation 1

'In a selling meeting we are expected to sell.' When asked the question, 'Who expects you to sell?' we get differing replies. These vary from:

1. 'Our organisation – we have new business development objectives to hit and we need to take every opportunity to sell our services.'

2. 'The client – the client wants to hear what you have got and what you can do to help.'

3. 'Me – if I see an opportunity I'm not going to let it go by.'

The common thread among all these replies is that there is a misunderstanding about what selling is. These professionals believe that selling is about talking. Talking is a *part* of selling but talking about the wrong things is a sure way to turn a prospective client into a client for one of our competitors.

Remember the chiropodist – perhaps he thought that his job was to sell.

Explanation 2

Another commonly heard explanation goes as follows: 'When you hear a client talk about a problem you can help them with, you naturally tell them then and there. You can't just sit and nod.'

In a well-tested simulation of a first meeting a conversation went like this:

Client   One of the things I want to get under way is our CDQ – Customer Driven Quality – programme. This has not been driven forward in the UK and we can make big improvements if we get it going.

Professional   Well we can probably help you there. We have experts in this field and we have supported many of our clients helping them to gain ISO9000 accreditation. I am sure we could also help you.

Client   No, we already have ISO9000. CDQ is an internal process. It's really about making the company totally client-focused.

Professional   Again we have expertise in this. We have worked with many major manufacturers like your company and helped them to devise and institute customer service programmes.

Client   Well it's really a bit more than a customer service programme. It begins by firstly developing the internal processes, ensuring that they are robust and are fully aligned with delivering ultimate customer satisfaction.

Professional   Oh, so it involves re-engineering some of your processes?

Client   I guess you could call it that.

Professional   Well we definitely can help. In addition to our expertise in ISO9000 and customer service development we do a lot of work in Business Process Re-engineering. Would you like to talk with one of our specialists in this area? I'm sure he could give you a lot of ideas.

Client   Well possibly he could – but my first priority is to recruit someone to take charge of the CDQ programme.

Professional   Do you have someone in mind?

Client   No, I'm going to have to go outside for this appointment.

Professional   We have an executive recruitment arm that could do this for you. They have an excellent track record in finding top people and I know they have recruited individuals in the service and quality fields.

Client   I've already got our personnel people working on this one. They are very good and I always use internal resources first time round when I'm looking to recruit. I've only ever used recruitment consultants when we've drawn a blank ourselves, and I have to say my experiences then weren't very favourable.

At this stage if the client begins to complain about his foot and his painful arch we can be fairly certain that the professional will begin to untie his shoelaces.

As Carlson says:

> . . . professionals – who may begin a sales interview by asking questions intended to uncover needs – often become side-tracked. As soon as the

prospect mentions something for which they have a solution, they snap at the bait and begin describing what they can do, usually in terms of 'Here's what we've done in situations similar to yours.' Not only do these people present a solution prematurely, but they deter the prospect from telling them more about their needs.

Explanation 3

A third reason given by some professionals being totally honest about first meetings, goes something along the following lines: 'When we're talking about his business there are many times when I'm on shaky ground. I like it when I can get the conversation onto something that I know about.'

A very honest explanation – but one which clearly has nothing to do with good selling practice. We may be very interested in a particular area of expertise. We may be very knowledgeable in our subject. However, if it has no apparent relevance to the prospective client, then it is of little value.

Most professionals we have ever worked with tell us that they do not want to be trained to become 'high pressure salesmen'. Yet the epitome of a high pressure salesman is the person who talks about his product and tries to sell his product to an unwilling customer. Unwittingly the untrained professional can demonstrate the very behaviours he or she would most seek to avoid.

The worst outcome from this type of behaviour results when the prospect reacts badly to being sold to. The prospect may start to raise objection after objection, she may even become personally objectionable. After the initial meeting she may become strangely unobtainable. The untrained professional can then draw the conclusion that 'selling' does not suit the professional arena and future 'selling' meetings develop into an apparently aimless and unstructured 'chat' where the main aim of the professional appears to be to do everything possible to avoid being seen to 'sell'.

HOW TO ASCERTAIN THE PROSPECTIVE CLIENT'S SITUATION AND REQUIREMENTS AND HOW TO CONFIRM YOUR UNDERSTANDING

To master the 'A' and the 'C' of the PACES process the professional needs to do three things well. He needs to:

1. Ask questions in the most effective manner.

2. Demonstrate that he can take the discussion logically forward by having listened and responded to what the client has said.

3. Choose the right questions for an effective 'Funnel' process.

The Funnel Process

A useful model which guides us through the first two of these three skill areas is the Funnel. The funnel is shown in Figure 7.1. You will see that the funnel process takes us smoothly from the 'A' (ascertaining the client's situation and requirements) into the 'C' of the PACES model (confirming our understanding of the client's situation and requirements).

Figure 7.1: The funnel process

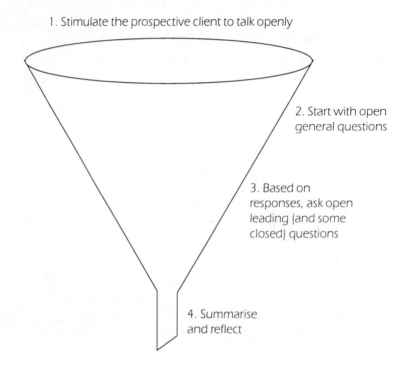

1. Stimulate the prospective client to talk openly

2. Start with open general questions

3. Based on responses, ask open leading (and some closed) questions

4. Summarise and reflect

The funnel works as follows:

1. We stimulate the prospective client to talk openly and answer our questions.

On scores of occasions we have seen professionals fail to get useful and detailed information from prospective clients even though they have prepared the questions they plan to ask and even though they use these prepared questions in the meeting. This can be very frustrating to the planned professional. One of the main reasons why the prospective client may not be forthcoming is explained as follows.

The professional knows he needs to ask questions very early in the meeting in order to identify needs and wants. He therefore prepares his questions and, as soon in the meeting as he can, he begins to bombard the client with his information-seeking 'missiles'.

The whole process is driven by what the professional wants and what the professional sees as being the 'logical' conduct and structure of the meeting. The client is not considered in the planning process.

Within minutes of the meeting starting, the client is being hit by questions, some of them in potentially sensitive areas, and she is typically thinking,

> 'Why does he need this information?' or,

> 'Where are we going with this?' or,

> 'I thought he said on the phone he wanted to come and talk about some ideas his firm had, how come he's just asking me for information?'

Sometimes it is patently clear from the expression on the prospective client's face that she is not comfortable with being questioned.

Often the questioning is interrupted by the client interjecting with something along the lines of,

> 'You said that your firm had expertise and ideas in this area. I think we've talked enough about my company. I'd like to know now what you can do for us.'

The professional has gained very little useful data up to this point. The answers which have been elicited have been brief to the point of being begrudging and now he is faced with the prospect of talking about his firm's products, services or capabilities without having any real understanding as to their applicability to the client to whom he is talking.

Most times this can be totally avoided by the use of the *stimulator* or *stimulating statement*. It is used before any questions are asked and is designed to explain to the prospective client why it is valuable for them to spend time answering questions and giving information.

An example could be:

> 'As I said a couple of minutes ago in my introduction, our firm has a very wide range of capabilities, however, rather than talk about generalities I would be keen to talk about services which could really help your business in the future. Whilst I've done some research into your company, by definition this research is dated and it also indicates little about the future.

> Could we therefore start off with me asking you a few questions to fill in some gaps and to understand where you see your organisation going? In that way we can then home in on those of our capabilities which you may consider appropriate and helpful.'

Given such an explanation or *stimulator* the prospective client understands the reason for the questions and can see a potential benefit in sharing information. We cannot remember a situation we have seen where a professional has used a powerful and well-expressed stimulator and has not been allowed to explore with questions.

The stimulator can be likened to putting a pound coin in a parking meter. It buys you time – in this case, questioning time.

2. Start with open general questions.

Most people have come across the concept of open and closed questions. It is considered by many to be 'old hat'. Training in questioning occurs (suitably) in many types of courses. Despite the intellectual simplicity of the concept it is surprising how superficial some understanding is.

Trainer to group	Have we come across the concept of open and closed questions before?
Response	Nods all round.
Trainer	OK, can someone tell me the difference between an open and a closed question?
Response	Yes, an open question is one which gives you a long answer. People can't answer it 'Yes' or 'No'.
Trainer	Right, but how would I know if I was looking at an open or a closed question? What would indicate this?
Response	Silence.
Trainer	I mean, if I looked at two questions written side by side, one open and one closed, what would be the structural difference?
Response	Silence.

Perhaps as the reader you know the answer. It is obvious. However, we have met many groups and individuals who profess to have been trained in questioning and who have 'temporarily forgotten' that the essential difference between an open question and a closed question is that an open question must begin with one of these words – *Who, What, Where, How, Why, When* or *Which*. If the question begins with any other word it is, by definition, a closed question and could be answered with one word – either 'Yes' or 'No'.

Why people tend to ask closed questions

Despite protestations by many, our observations over the years prove that most people have poor ability in asking open questions. There are a number of explanations suggested as to why this is so. Among these are:

Explanation 1

It is easier to ask a closed question as there are only seven ways of beginning an open question. This is undoubtedly so. A closed question could begin with the words 'Can', 'Do', 'Have', 'Will', 'Shall', 'May', 'Are', 'Is', 'Could', 'Should', etc., plus all the negatives of these words (e.g. 'Can't', 'Won't' and so on).

Explanation 2

It has been noted for years that very young children have the ability to ask very open questions. Those of us who have had children will recall the sometimes unending question 'Why?' It is as if a young child's brain is like blotting paper – it wants to absorb as much as it can. However, as children start to develop an understanding of their world, their questioning changes.

Instead of 'Why?' the question becomes, 'Why does it do that, Dad? Is it because . . . ?' The child is trying to see if the answer fits into its model of the world. The most comfortable answer is one in which the parent replies in some way to the affirmative.

Most closed questions indicate very clearly the line of response which the questioner would feel most comfortable in receiving. However, such questions are extremely limited as a means of information gathering and do very little to help us to really understand the other person and their position.

Explanation 3

Explanation 3 is sometimes expressed in the following way:

> 'All this stuff about open and closed questions is theoretical. Most of the time you ask a closed question people tell you a lot more than "Yes" or "No". In fact I know people whom I have a hard time shutting up no matter what sort of question I ask them! I don't see the point in practising all this open questioning stuff.'

This is a weak excuse – usually given after observation has proven that the individual concerned rarely asks open questions.

Of course there are people who will talk no matter what the question. Equally there are other people who are more reticent and who have to be asked the sorts of questions which will encourage them to 'open up'. The individual who continuously uses only closed questions will not fare very well in opening up others who have to be 'drawn'.

The argument that closed questions work as well as open questions is like a golfer saying he does not practise with his sand wedge as he never gets into a bunker. All golfers would like to think this could be the case but the reality is that in difficult situations one needs expertise with all of the clubs in the bag. Not all golf is played on the greens and not all clients are loquacious.

The difference between open general and open leading questions

Step 2 of the Funnel process says to begin with open general questions and Step 3 then goes on to say that we follow up with open leading and closed questions. So what is the difference between an open general and an open leading question?

Initially the two question types look very similar. Both open general and open leading questions begin with the 'W' words – Who, What, Why, Where, When, How and Which.

However, an open general question will usually give a response which is uninfluenced by the question which is being asked. An open leading questions will receive an answer which may have been influenced by the question.

For example, two questions which could form part of a meeting designed to get to understand a client's business and its production processes could be:

'What effects have the new packaging regulations had on your business?'

'What problems have the new packaging regulations caused for your business?'

There is a subtle but significant difference in the questions. The first question has a far wider scope. The question seeks to understand what effects – good, bad and indifferent – the regulations have had. The second question only concerns itself with the negative aspects – the problems. The person answering the question is led to talk about problems.

Over the years we have had people argue that the second question is the more effective. After all, they claim, the professional is in the meeting to find out what the problems are and to provide solutions. The unfortunate reality is that a client knows when she has been asked a leading question – and can choose to react accordingly.

There does not need to be a debate as to which question is better – in a good meeting probably both will be used. However, there is a *best order* for using the two questions.

The first question – the more open of the two – should be used first. This is for two reasons. Firstly it is less likely to be create a defensive reaction from the client. This is because there is less vested interest (i.e. 'problems') in the question. Secondly the question is more likely to provide a wider information trawl.

Imagine the meeting:

Professional   What effects have the new packaging regulations had on your business?

Client   Well they forced us to look hard at how we packaged all of our lines. It was something we hadn't done seriously for years. We decided that we should take a genuinely creative look at our packaging. We used experts from both in house and outside to come up with ideas, and in the next few months we will be launching some exciting new lines utilising innovative packaging processes.

On the surface of it, this response may not seem like good news to the professional – *but it is the real picture*. The professional needs to keep exploring (funnelling) – understanding more and more of the picture. At an appropriate time in the meeting he may be able to come back with:

Professional   You have said that the new packaging, whilst very attractive, is less regular in shape than the old traditional lines; what problems does that bring you?

The 'problems' question (in which the professional may have a vested interest) is now positioned differently. It has been asked in context and it has been asked in an informed way – based on the knowledge which the client has given to the professional in the preceding part of the meeting.

Again, our observations over the years demonstrate that even when people do ask open questions, the majority are open leading questions and are leading at too early a stage in the meeting. It seems we can't resist asking questions which tell the other person how we want them to answer. Unfortunately most people resist strongly being led by questions – to the point that some will even lie in order to provide their questioner with an answer he does not want to hear!

Open Leading questions have a very important function in any meeting. They are the sort of questions which are most likely to give substance to the opportunities, issues and problems which will provide a professional with work. We must just make sure that they are used at the appropriate time. As in courtship, the ardent suitor may want to get down to the kissing and cuddling as soon as possible. However, courtship requires a period of getting to know you and hand-holding may need to precede any more intimate contact.

Going in for the early 'kill' with leading questions is a sure way to raise client resistance and cause the client to mistrust our motives.

Can one, therefore, classify questions as either open general or open leading? Every person we have seen attempting this has ended up in an intellectual debate with people trying to prove that his open general question is really somewhat leading. The answer is that all open questions live somewhere on a continuum stretching from totally open and general at one end to open but extremely leading at the other. (See Figure 7.2.)

Figure 7.2:   The open question continuum

Totally open
general
questions

Totally leading
specific
questions

The one guideline which can be applied with some degree of accuracy is that a very open and general question will usually be short and contain very few words whereas a question (almost by definition) becomes more leading as it becomes longer.

In the funnelling process the aim is to start the discussion on any subject (funnel) with some good open general questions and then to listen to what is said (and not said) and to follow up with other open questions based on the picture which is being built up. As we seek to define more detail in the picture, the questions have to become more specific and so the skilled practitioner 'naturally' makes the conversion from asking open general questions to open leading questions. Closed questions will also be used in the information-gathering part of the meeting where we are tying down details.

Encouraging open responses through good listening

A good meeting in which we are ascertaining the prospective client's situation and requirements should not appear to the client as a question and answer session. A good meeting should seem more like a logical free-flowing discussion – but with the client doing most of the talking. In order to achieve this the professional must move the meeting along based on the responses to the questions which he has prepared before the meeting. This can only be achieved if the professional has actually listened to the answers which the client has provided. More importantly, the professional must demonstrate to the other person that they are really listening. It matters not a jot that we have total recall of everything which is said in a meeting if it appears to the other person that we are not showing interest during the meeting itself. If we appear not to be paying close attention, people will very quickly cease to give us information.

We must therefore have the ability both to really understand what the other person is saying and 'where they are coming from' and also to demonstrate this. The way in which this is achieved is simply through listening. The word 'simply' is a misnomer. For many of us proficiency in this skill is far from simple. Demonstrating that we are listening takes a number of forms which range from being quite passive to the point where we demonstrate active listening.

Demonstrating our listening

Staying silent

This is the most passive way of showing we are prepared to listen. We simply let the other person talk and do not attempt to interrupt them. Simple as it may seem there are some who find this difficult. The old adage goes, 'Some people listen, others wait to talk.' When we meet people who wait to talk it becomes very evident quite quickly. These people always seem a little distant when we are talking to them as they are really in the process of forming their response rather than listening to what we have to say.

Using positive body language

There are signs which indicate that we are listening. Conversely there are signs which indicate that we are not. A good listener will deliberately manifest signs that she is listening. A posture of slightly leaning forward, head turned a shade to one side (turning one ear toward the speaker), good eye contact and appropriately timed nodding of the head in understanding, give the speaker the clear feedback that his spoken message is being paid close attention.

We have never met anyone who told us that they deliberately used negative, discouraging body language – so is there any point in mentioning the subject? The fact that no one deliberately uses 'non-listening' body language does not mean that it is not used. Most people in most meetings are unaware of their body language. It is unfortunately common to see people displaying 'neutral' (at best) body language in meetings with clients.

Video tapes of role-plays also bear out this conclusion. The person who really looks as though she is interested is one step ahead of the person who hasn't got a clue how she looks to the prospective client.

The message is clear. Demonstrate positive, listening body language and do it consciously.

Using encouraging words, phrases and 'noises'

We are all familiar with these devices. They are words like 'Really?' – said with the inflection of the voice being raised at the end of the word – and phrases like 'Go on!' 'Uh huh', and 'Mmmmm' are two examples which fall into the 'noises' category.

Such expressions are usually accompanied by raised eyebrows, a widening of the eyes and other positive body language indicators which are all saying to the speaker, 'I am listening. I am interested. I want to hear more of what you have to say.'

Whilst we are all familiar with these devices some people get more value from them because they employ them more often. It is hard to overuse this simple device unless one develops a clichéd approach. Using 'You don't say' ten times in a row could cause the speaker to retort with, 'Yes, I do say!'

The key is to vary the expression.

Taking notes

Taking notes in business meetings is quite the accepted norm. The person who fails to take notes is the odd person out today and we have often heard people remark negatively about another person who has participated in a detailed meeting and not taken one note throughout. The excuses are as plausible as they are predictable.

'I wanted to give the meeting my full attention and I can't write and listen.'

'If you're writing notes you can't maintain eye contact. It appears that you're more interested in writing than listening.'

People who make such remarks are either poor note-takers or are not really interested in what the other person has to say, despite protestations to the contrary. As note-taking is an accepted demonstration of paying attention it is up to us to learn how to carry out this function. We dress smartly for business meetings as this is the socially accepted thing to do. Similarly we need to be able to perform the socially accepted skill of note-taking.

Note-taking does not mean taking down everything which is said *verbatim*. A good note-taker will jot down the significant details emerging from a meeting into a format which he or she will be able to use after the meeting has finished. Like any skill it needs practice and with practice it will develop into a good habit.

Unbundling key words and phrases

We have had people in the past tell us that all of the above ways of demonstrating listening can be faked. Nod, look interested, scribble a few things onto a piece of paper and say, 'That's interesting' a few times and you have it made. We would suggest that this is a rather dangerous strategy and that people are observant enough to realise the fake from the genuine article.

However, unbundling is not something which can be faked. Unbundling can only be carried out by someone who is paying attention, listening closely and trying to genuinely understand what the other person is trying to communicate.

It could go something like this:

Client	We have developed our forecasting systems so that shortfalls or overstocking are not usually a problem.
Professional	Usually?
Client	Yes, 85 to 90 per cent of our orders are for existing products. Where we do sometimes have a hiccup is with new products.
Professional	New products?
Client	Our traditional lines have been emulated by many of our competitors and therefore to stay ahead we are increasingly having to develop new product ranges.
Professional	From what you're saying then, even though the problem is not great now, it is likely to grow?
Client	Probably – unless we can find ways of predicting the volumes of these new lines more accurately.

What started out as an unpromising line from the client has turned into a potential need on which the professional may be able to offer assistance. The opportunity occurred because the professional was listening very closely to what the client said.

There is no reason why a person we are talking with for the first time should trust us to the point where they will tell us everything. We totally unburden ourselves only to those people in whom we choose to trust. However, there are often words which people will use which may seem insignificant in themselves but which may be the tip of a very important iceberg.

'We are *quite* satisfied' could mean that there are a number of aspects about which we are not happy.

'We will not pursue the subject *at this point in time*' could mean that there is a date at which the subject *will* be reviewed.

'There is *considerable* opinion that we should take this next step' could mean that there are some significant voices in opposition who are not yet convinced.

So often such words and expressions pass us by. We decide they are not particularly significant or meaningful and do not explore by unbundling.

The professional who is a good unbundler demonstrates very markedly that he is determined to *really* understand – not to just understand the position from a superficial point of view. Unbundling produces a virtuous circle. By unbundling we demonstrate that we want to understand. By demonstrating that we want to understand, the client will be motivated to be more forthcoming in the detail of the information which she chooses to share with us.

Another significant reason for unbundling is that some people do not explain themselves clearly at all times.

For example:

Professional   You described earlier the main objectives your organisation has for the future. How will you go about achieving these objectives?

Client   Well, we haven't exactly been sitting on our hands, you know. We have already done a lot of work and we are quite a way down the road with a number of projects related to improving our marketing tools. Do you know what I mean?

The temptation is to say, 'Yes I know what you mean – of course!' We fear appearing stupid if we reply to the effect that we don't understand. However, what the client has said is not clear at all. If she was talking to a person within her own organisation that other person would probably know what she meant by 'marketing tools', would probably know how many projects there were and what they were about and may even know how far 'down the road' they were.

The professional must begin to unpick and unbundle.

Professional   Broadly speaking, yes . . . but I am not totally clear on what you include as 'marketing tools' in your particular company. What are these?

Unbundling is a skill demonstrated by a good listener – but this does not yet qualify us to claim to be an active listener.

Figure 7.3:   Listening

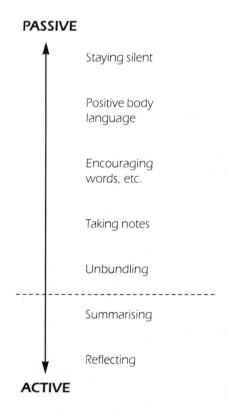

PASSIVE

Staying silent

Positive body language

Encouraging words, etc.

Taking notes

Unbundling

Summarising

Reflecting

ACTIVE

Active listening

The fourth stage of the funnel process is to summarise and reflect. This is the demonstration of Active Listening. An active listener not only demonstrates all of the previous listening skills, he is able to *give feedback* through summarising the facts and content of the messages spoken by the client and reflecting on any feelings which may have been associated with the message.

Summarising

A question we have been asked innumerable times over the years is:

> 'How do I know when I've reached the bottom of a funnel? I explore a subject with a client and when I think I understand I leave it and move on to something else. A bit later on in the meeting it becomes evident that there is more I needed to know about the first subject and I have to jump back to it. The meeting gets really messy and unstructured.'

This type of problem is one we witness almost daily. The resultant 'mess' we term 'funnel hopping' – jumping from subject to subject in an almost random way. The remedy is to carry out the fourth part of the funnel process. When we believe we are at the bottom of a funnel (i.e. we believe that we have the full picture) we should summarise our understanding. A number of immense benefits emanate from this practice. These are:

- Having to summarise really does make us work to *understand* what the client has been saying.

- The act of summarising often causes us to realise that we cannot complete the summary because *we lack certain information* – hence another question is prompted.

- *We eliminate errors and misunderstandings* because the other person will correct these. These misunderstandings may or may not be our 'fault'. It could be that the client has expressed herself poorly or in an incomplete manner. Fault is of no consequence to the summary. All we are attempting to do is to ensure that our understanding of the information is the same as that which the client has been trying to communicate.

- We give the client a *powerful demonstration* that we are listening and are making every attempt to understand what she has to say.

- If our summary is incomplete *the client will usually fill in the gaps* and add more information – enabling us to more adequately finish off a funnel.

A complaint which is voiced of some clients is:

> 'He keeps repeating himself. I understand first time round but he feels he has to tell me another four times.'

If you have this problem with some people, try using a summary after they have imparted information to you. In this way they will *know* that you understand rather than being unsure and feeling that repetition will reinforce their message.

There is some misunderstanding about summarising. We have observed people who were told they were good at summarising because after an hour's meeting they spent 30 seconds at the end summarising the agreements of the discussion and the way forward. Whilst this is good practice this is not the summarising associated with active listening. Nor, after speaking about her accounting process for 20 minutes is the professional's 'summary' of the client's processes amounting to, 'So, all in all, it works pretty well then.'

Whilst a summary should not be a parrot-fashion repetition of what has been said, it must contain a paraphrased interpretation of the key facts – demonstrating that the information has been heard, interpreted and stored reasonably accurately.

Every meeting will be different but a good active listener will summarise every five or ten minutes – and sometimes more often than this.

Reflecting

Few people speak for any length of time using 'digital' language. By digital we mean language where the words convey messages but there is no indication of any emotion associated with the words being used. All research indicates that this is not the case. In one piece of research carried out by Mehrabian the conclusions were that only 10 per cent of the message as understood by the recipient was due to the words which were used. The 90 per cent balance was transmitted through the tone of voice used and the body language associated with the message as it was being spoken.

Despite having up to 90 per cent of the message adding context and meaning to the words being used, it is a rare person who reflects this back to the speaker – demonstrating that not only has the message been noted and understood, but that the listener also knows 'where the other person is coming from'.

For example:

'You are obviously very passionate about this project . . .'

'I sense that you are slightly apprehensive about the next step . . .'

'I get the impression that even though you were angry, there is also a touch of sadness . . .'

'Clearly you are enthusiastic about this . . .'

Passion, apprehension, anger, sadness and enthusiasm are examples of emotions which may come across as part of the message. Reflecting tells the other person that we recognise how they *feel* about the subject in question.

In talking with salespeople over the years and asking them what they hope to achieve in early meetings with customers it is common to hear the objective, 'I try to sell myself first'. When asked, 'So how do you achieve this?' a typical reply is, 'I try to build rapport and empathy with the customer.' When further pursued with the question, 'So how do you actually build rapport and empathy?' the quality of answers usually erodes rapidly into comments about finding out what sports the other person is interested in and talking about that.

We once saw empathy well described as:

'Putting yourself in another's shoes without wanting to wear them.'

Dedicating the concentration and effort to really try to understand how the other person feels, to the point of verbalising this, is the most effective way of demonstrating to a prospective client that you really want to build empathy, rapport and trust.

Active listening proficiency

So how good is the average professional as an active listener? Indeed how proficient is the average salesperson who regularly claims to want to build empathy and rapport? Whilst clearly there are exceptions, the average is somewhere between mediocre and poor. Perhaps we should not be surprised.

During our early lives we are taught all of the communication skills – bar one. We are taught by our parents how to talk, we are taught how to read and write. Most people who participate in our training courses, however, have never had any lessons or training in listening skills. Being told to listen in class and being punished for not doing so hardly counts as a lesson in communication skills in our assessment.

People who express themselves well using the spoken or written word do so because they work hard at the proficiencies of these media. They study and they practise and they combine this skills development with whatever natural talent they are fortunate enough to possess. Proficient speed-readers do the same. To become proficient listeners we need the motivation to want to be well above the mediocre. With the motivation in place we stand some chance of devoting the effort and energy into achieving a communication ability possessed by all too few.

● ●

Active Listening – a Case Study

The power of active listening was once demonstrated to us by a colleague with whom we worked in a previous company. Mark had been responsible for co-ordinating the training of a group of senior managers from the European subsidiaries of a large US high-tech company. The training had gone very well and the MD of the UK company told Mark he was so convinced that he wanted to use us to carry out sales training in the UK. The MD (as was his wont) made this decision without consulting his three senior divisional sales managers. They were told after the decision had been made and were given a fait accompli.

I was appointed as the trainer for the UK group and the day arrived when we had to carry out our first research into the UK client company. I picked up Mark in the morning and as we drove to the client's HQ he expressed his concern that the divisional sales managers might be somewhat hostile toward us due to the autocratic way in which the training of their sales staff had been decided.

As Mark had all of the connections and knowledge of the client organisation, it was agreed that he would take the lead in the three meetings we had scheduled (one with each of the sales managers). I would take a fairly low-key role.

The first meeting was at 10 o'clock. The atmosphere was almost icy. My colleague sat opposite the sales manager who was jacketed and in position behind his large desk. I sat slightly behind and to one side of Mark. It would have been easy for Mark to hide behind the MD's decision and to take the line that it was a fait accompli for us all therefore we had better just get on with it. He didn't. He made every effort to really listen to what the first sales manager had to say. He demonstrated this through active listening. He summarised regularly to make sure that he had understood and to demonstrate that he wanted to understand.

From time to time he reflected the feelings and concerns of the sales manager – demonstrating that he understood how the sales manager felt about the various subjects we discussed. Expressions such as 'So how you see it is . . .' and 'So your feelings are . . .' were a regular feature of the meeting.

After about 30 minutes the atmosphere had changed significantly. Mark and the sales manager were physically closer together. The sales manager drew diagrams and small charts on his pad to explain things which Mark was clearly interested in. Mark had to move into such a position that he could see. The sales manager was by this stage quite comfortable with this. The body language which had started as rather formal and stilted became more expansive and relaxed.

At the end of an hour and a half there had clearly been a meeting of minds and one opponent was now open to our involvement in his sales training – if not yet an advocate.

The second meeting was a re-run of the first. A defensive and totally unconvinced person at the start was 'converted' over the next 90 minutes.

We had lunch and Mark and I met with the third of the sales managers. Though not quite as 'stiff' as his other two colleagues, he would have proven a tough nut for most people. The 'magic' of active listening worked again. In the late afternoon we were on our way back down the motorway with the UK client's most influential people supporting the training which their people were to receive and believing that those who were going to carry it out really understood what was needed and why.

After a few minutes in the car I turned to Mark and asked him a question. He did not reply. The reason was simple. He was asleep. He was mentally exhausted from the three meetings. For the best part of five hours he had turned up his active listening skills to a very high pitch. That requires motivation, effort and mental stamina.

❋ ❋

A scarce skill

Almost everyone who understands what active listening is, wants to become good at it. However, few people work on developing it to any level of proficiency. We may be wrong but we believe that one reason why really good active listening is such a scarce skill is that it does require such a lot of mental energy. It is all to easy to nod and say, 'Yeah, I understand.'

The rarest and finest of skills all take work to master. It is only by application and practice that we will improve. A theoretical understanding of the skill is only the beginning.

Most importantly the benefits of active listening will only be fully delivered if we approach the skill as one which is designed to help us help others. If we see active listening as a technique to enable us to manipulate and gain advantage we should not be surprised if people 'spot the technique' and see us as behaving in an unnatural and false way. Instead of building empathy and trust, the application of the skills as a pure technique will erode the very thing we seek to build.

CHOOSING QUESTIONS FOR AN EFFECTIVE FUNNEL PROCESS

The 'Business' funnels

If we are to sell a service or capability which we claim will benefit the client's organisation, it is imperative that we first of all understand the client's business. Whilst decision-makers may have personal agendas which affect their decisions (something we will address further in Section 5) any decision to use professional advice has to be justified to shareholders and employees on rational, logical grounds. Therefore clients are not going to invest in buying services which fail to add value to *their* specific business.

Very early in the meeting we must find out where the prospective client's business is today and where it has come from in the past. Most importantly however, we must ascertain where the business is heading in the future. We cannot repair the problems of yesterday, and the problems and opportunities of today are probably already being addressed. Where opportunity is most likely to lie is in the unfulfilled opportunities, unresolved problems and unaddressed issues which are on the horizon.

Questions about the business can be asked in three tenses – past, present and future. It is an established fact that the individuals who are most successful at selling ask more of their questions in the future tense. Obvious, when one thinks about it!

For the future a prospective client may want to:

- Be more cost-effective.
- Be more timely in responding to its customers.
- Increase its business volumes.
- Reduce its working capital.
- Make more qualified decisions.
- Be more competitive in its current place.
- Portray a better image.
- Reduce staff turnover.
- Attract the best people in the marketplace.

- Reduce time to market.

- Comply with impending legislation.

These are examples of business issues. Prospective clients have two ways of addressing these types of issue. Firstly they can deal with them utilising their own resources. Alternatively they can employ outside expertise. However, we cannot fully understand the issue, the size of the issue and its potential impact if we do not firstly understand where these issues lie in relation to the future direction of the business.

For instance, reducing time to market for new products may be an issue for a prospective client company. How significant an issue it will be, will be determined by factors such as:

- How demanding the market will be for new products.

- The types of customers the company will be supplying in the future.

- The numbers of new products which the company is likely to have to produce in the future.

- The likely responsiveness of future competitors.

- The plans which the company already has in place to shorten time to market.

The professional needs to understand this market and company background as early as possible. Whilst a professional may be a market specialist and therefore have a good grasp of the market situation, what he does not know is the prospective client's:

- Perception of the market.

- Business.

- Perception of her own business.

The third factor is extremely important. No study of information and no amount of planning can determine the individual client's perception. The professional with all of the statistics in the world at his fingertips can approach a prospective client who he knows is falling behind the game in terms of (by way of example) time to market. However, if the perception of the individuals within this organisation is that this is not an important issue then he will struggle to convince them that this is so.

People within the prospective client organisation may argue that the perceived wisdom of the pundits is invalid because:

- They suffer from management myopia. They can see, touch and feel past and current successes but have no processes for envisioning a different future.

- There may be a series of even bigger problems which may need more urgent resolution.

- The time-to-market issue may in itself only be a symptom of a bigger problem.

- Management may have plans in place to resolve the problem.

Research information is always out of date. The only question is how far out of date it is.

The conclusion we draw again is that the only way to really understand the perceived business issues and the positioning of these issues is to ask the key individuals within the prospective client organisation.

In numerous surveys carried out with business customers into their attitudes towards suppliers, the biggest shortcoming of salespeople has been summed up by customers as:

'They don't understand my business.'

The perception of the salespeople invariably differs in this respect. However, salespeople don't make the buying decisions and they don't sign the cheques. The perception of the customer, or client, is the only important perception. Providers of professional services are under an even greater obligation by the very nature of their offering to really understand the client, how the business operates and where it is going in the future. In a competitive marketplace we cannot afford to run the risk of being accused of not understanding our clients' businesses.

We cannot plan every question which we will ask in an exploratory early meeting. However, we can plan the broad subjects into which we would wish to delve. In other words we can plan the 'funnel opening' questions – the open general questions which start the free flow of information.

Some examples of funnel opening questions which could be asked

- How is your company positioned today?
- What are the biggest pressures in your market today?
- What will be the issues in your marketplace in the future?
- What are the likely changes you are going to have to face in the future?
- What are the issues for your organisation in dealing with future changes?
- What are your key business objectives in the foreseeable future?
- What are the main strategies that you will employ to achieve these objectives?
- What plans do you have to increase your competitiveness in the future?
- What impact will your strategies have on the size and shape of your organisation?
- What is your current organisational structure?
- In the light of your future strategy, what path or strategy are you considering for:
  - IT?
  - Manpower?
  - Financial management?
  - Sales?
  - Marketing?
  - Taxation issues?
  - Distribution?
  - Product development?
  - R & D?
  - (name your own subject area)

For the professional in IT or marketing – or any other expertise area – the final question is the one we want to hear answered. This is the one where there may be opportunity and work. Whilst there is no specific order in which these example funnel openers should be posed, we would recommend that the 'self-interest' question at the bottom is definitely the last of these types of questions to be asked. By the time we have explored all of the preceding funnels we should be developing a clear understanding of the client's perception of the future of her organisation and where the gaps and opportunities lie.

Another valid reason for taking the discussion down this route is the often-quoted observation that people love to talk about their businesses and they like to talk on their agenda. We feel less comfortable – and sometimes manipulated – when people want to get onto *their* agenda straight away. In following the suggested route the professional is demonstrating interest in the client – a step toward establishing compatibility and ultimately building a feeling of trust.

Demonstrating competence through questions

David Maister in his article 'How Clients Choose' writes:

> I discount all your assertions about your expertise until you give me some evidence to back them up. For example don't tell me about your experience in my industry (or on a particular topic). Rather, illustrate it by asking questions that reveal your knowledge of key industry terminology, facts and latest figures or latest events. That way, I'll draw my own conclusions (which I'm going to do anyway) about how well you understand my business and my issues.

The examples of funnel openers in the previous section are deliberately written in an open general style. This is mainly for simplicity. From time to time we have had people protest about the format of these questions. Their main point is that the questions may sound extremely naive to the potential client – particularly if the meeting was positioned with the professional being some kind of industry specialist. The comments are valid. However, we must take care not to lose the value of a question which is open and as wide-scoping as possible.

When finding out about a prospective client's business it is important to preface some questions with *competence builders*.

If talking with a prospect in the banking sector a question you may wish to ask could be:

> 'What do you see as the main issues impacting on your business today and in the future?'

This may better be expressed as:

> 'A number of our clients are finding that with the upturn in the economy and the resolution of the worst of the bad book issues generated in the late 1980s, there appears to be an increasing focus on increasing the asset base. Clearly this puts pressures into the market and drives down margins.

That is one issue we're seeing but I'd be interested to know what you see as the main factors impacting upon your business today and into the future?'

The prefix sentences imply that we know about her industry – without any attempt to air our 'expert opinion'. At the end of the question the prospect is left to express her own thoughts.

Another example – this time the prospect is a £35 million turnover computer systems integrator.

'The industry has had for many years to live with slim margins on hardware – and software is also moving rapidly to being a commodity offering.

What plans do you have for your company given these difficult market conditions?'

This question illustrates more competence than:

'What plans do you have for the future?'

Competence builders must preface the question – not be added as a suffix. There is a great danger that a wrongly expressed question:

- Turns into an example of the professional trying to impress with his knowledge instead of trying to seek information from the prospective client.

- Is seen by the client as a deliberate attempt to lead her in a specific direction into which she may not wish to go – or to get her to express opinions she genuinely does not support.

- Ends up with the professional supplying the answer himself.

For example:

'What do you see as the issues which will impact upon your business plans in the future? . . . For instance how do you see the impending EC green legislation affecting the way you do business? . . . Do you think that this is going to make life more difficult for you and raise your costs? . . . I guess it has to doesn't it?'

What was intended as a good information-seeking question ends up as a rhetorical question. The prospective client really does not need to be consulted. A nod of the head will suffice if a question is posed in this way – hardly conducive to the open dialogue and rapport we are seeking to build in an early meeting with a prospect.

Multiple choice questions

The last example is also an example of what is called the multiple choice question. We have asked people who have a tendency to ask a lot of these types of questions why this is so. They give a number of reasons including:

- They are not sure that they have made the question very clear.

- They think of a better (sometimes unconnected!) question as they are putting their first attempt into words.

- They believe that the client does not understand the question.

- When the client pauses for thinking time the questioner 'loses his nerve' in the short silence and continues by embellishing the question.

- In their heart of hearts they want the client to agree with them so they give enough clues in the questions as to what is the 'correct' answer.

Whatever the reason for the multiple choice question it is a demonstration of poor information-seeking. Imagine a prospective client on the end of this multiple choice effort:

> 'So where do you see your company in five years' time? I mean what are your objectives as an organisation? . . . Will you have to expand into the new market areas or will you seek to focus in particular niches where you have relatively greater strength? For instance, what about your field service commitment – will you continue to develop this when products are ever more disposable? . . . Do you have plans yourselves to produce a long-life disposable range?'

When finally given the chance, where does the prospective client start? There are some interesting questions wrapped up (and lost) in this illustration. In all good faith the client may start with the last part of the question – talking about the merits and demerits of long-life disposable products. From our observations the rest of the questions are probably lost for ever.

The worst case scenario is when the professional, upon reviewing the meeting, states something to the effect of:

> 'I asked her about her company's future objectives and she never gave me an answer.'

CHOOSING QUESTIONS FOR AN EFFECTIVE FUNNEL PROCESS

The 'Offer Analysis' funnels

Creating the offer analysis

Once there has been an in-depth discussion drawn out from following the 'Business' funnels, it is appropriate and logical to move the discussion closer to the specific area in which the professional has particular expertise. The final question under the heading 'Some examples of funnel opening questions which could be asked' (page 114) begins to move in this direction. The exploration of the business issues may in itself begin to surface opportunities and problems in which the professional has expertise.

Before we begin to state how we could be of assistance to the client we must firstly establish how close a match there is between what appears to be the client's requirements and what the professional's organisation can deliver. Again we cannot predict every question we may need to ask to establish the match between the client's requirements and the professional's capabilities. We can again however determine the funnel openers – those open general questions which get us into the key areas which need exploration.

There is a simple tool which we use for this. It is called the Offer Analysis. An Offer Analysis can have a number of dimensions. For the purpose of determining what questions we need to use as funnel openers we will keep this tool to its most basic two-dimensional format.

We take a piece of A4 paper and divide it down the middle. On the left hand side of the sheet we list all of the features of the product, service or capability which the firm could offer to a prospective client.

The definition of a feature is: Any fact about our potential offering to a client.

On the right hand side of the sheet of paper we list all of the funnel openers which will help us explore what relevance the feature has to the particular prospective client to whom we are speaking.

We have worked with numerous clients constructing Offer Analyses. No matter how detailed and apparently complex the product or capability, we have found that it is unusual to need more than nine funnel opening questions. Remember, this does not mean that we will only ask nine questions or fewer. What it means is that there are nine or fewer subject areas which we need to explore to determine the fit between what we can do and what the client requires. In each area we have the funnel opener formulated.

Using the Offer Analysis

On page 119 we have an example of an Offer Analysis formulated for a fictitious IT consultancy. The features are not listed in any particular order. The questions are listed in a *potential* 'batting order'. We stress the word 'potential' because when one asks an open general question the ensuing funnelling process can take us down any number of unpredictable avenues.

The answer to the question, 'What will your future IT platform look like?' may very quickly and logically cause the client to talk about future projects. Clearly this makes the funnel opener, 'What projects are planned for the future?' completely redundant.

The third column on this example indicates the features which could be assessed by exploring in depth the funnel opened by the question listed in column two.

There are three separate questions which could ascertain the value of this consultancy's geographical location to a potential client. However, if we find out that a prospective client only has offices in one city and has no intention of establishing any of its future IT infrastructure outside of this one location, then this is a feature which delivers no benefit – to this particular prospect.

Professionals unskilled in the selling process tend to stress the points about their firm which *they* see as being strengths or unique points. Unless these features deliver a potential benefit to the client, talking about them is a waste of breath. Emphasis on such points usually has the opposite effect to the one intended. In the scenario of the client only having one location, what could be the reaction of the prospective client who is listening to the consultant talk about his company's expanding geographical empire? Probably she is thinking something along the lines of:

'All these offices are of no consequence to me and they must cost a lot of money to run. I think if we need some help with the next IT project we should use someone who is local.'

Exploring the areas opened up by the Offer Analysis funnel openers enables us to focus our offer on those features in which the client will see value.

Table 7.1: Offer Analysis for IT Consultancy Services Limited

	Features	Questions	Features explored
1	130 full-time consultants	What is your current and future IT platform?	5,6,7
2	Access to 250 specialist associates		
3	Ten offices around the UK	Where is it today and where will it be located in the future?	3,4
4	Offices in Paris, Bonn, Brussels		
5	Project experience of all major hardware vendors	What projects are planned for the future?	3,4,5,6,7, 9,12
6	Project experience of all major integrated software packages	How will/should these projects be approached and managed?	13,14,15, 16
7	Data and Tele Comms expertise/capability		
8	Wide industry sector experience	What internal capability/ capacity do you possess?	1,2,3,4,10, 11,13,14
9	Capability to produce bespoke software	Who will be affected by future IT projects and developments?	16
10	Consultants with IT backgrounds		
11	Consultants with: – Financial – Manufacturing – Logistics backgrounds/experience	What timescales will the projects have to meet?	1,2,13,15
12	'Runaway systems' expertise	What do you seek from an outside source of assistance?	1 to 15
13	Proven Project Management methodology and tools		
14	Proven methodology and tools for software selection and implementation		
15	Proven concurrent engineering tools/processes		
16	Experience of managing change caused by IT developments		

THE MEETING SO FAR

Let us now summarise the points covered so far and put them in the context of the whole meeting. We have gone through the following stages:

1. We have positioned ourselves and our organisation at the beginning of the meeting. We have outlined what we see as the aims and format of the meeting and have ascertained if the client has any additional agenda points.

2. We have used the *stimulator* at the beginning of our questioning to explain to the prospective client the reasons for our searching questions and the value to her of answering these questions.

3. We have developed an understanding of the prospective client's business and the issues it faces by exploring the 'Business' funnels.

4. We have moved on to explore any potential fit between what the prospective client may require and our organisation's capabilities by exploring the funnels suggested by creating an Offer Analysis.

We are forming a framework for the initial meeting – not a rigid straitjacket. The questions described above must not become a 'questionnaire' which the professional uses to interrogate the prospective client. They become an *aide memoire* which the professional has to hand, to use as necessary. Preparing in this way helps to ensure that:

•   The 'best' questions are asked, not just the best ones that come to mind at the time.

•   The professional gathers as comprehensive a level of information as time allows – no key areas are missed.

•   The professional does not need to use precious mental energy in thinking of the next funnel opener. He can relax and focus all of his attention on listening to and understanding the prospective client's replies and on 'funnelling' these replies skilfully.

To work well within this framework the professional needs to be very flexible – particularly in responding to the answers which emanate from the initial funnel opening questions. He must be able to adapt to the information he receives. He must be capable of picking up the signals – both spoken and unspoken. He must be capable of summarising his understanding of the client's position at the drop of a hat and should be able to reflect accurately the client's feelings.

As in developing any skill, the professional needs to study and understand what best practice looks like. From there the next step is to practise.

Figure 7.4: Planning the subjects to explore

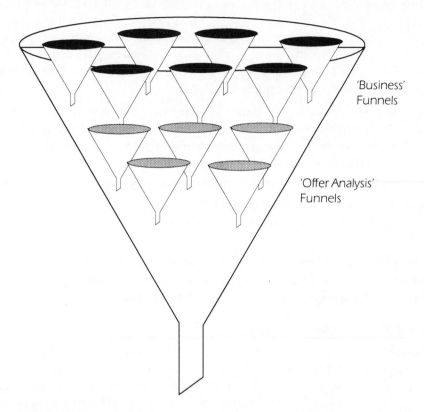

'Business'
Funnels

'Offer Analysis'
Funnels

CHOOSING QUESTIONS FOR AN EFFECTIVE FUNNEL PROCESS

The 'Commercial' funnels

If ever there was a set of questions which professionals fail to ask or tend to avoid asking, it is the 'Commercial' funnel openers. How do we know this? On hundreds of seminars professionals tell us this is so. These same people also give us anecdote after anecdote relating to the problems and failures they have been involved in by failing to explore these issues.

There are five commercial areas to explore. They are:

1. The Basis of Decision (BOD).

2. The money or budgetary issues.

3. The competitive situation.

4. The timescales.

5. The Decision-making Process (DMP).

Why do people avoid these issues? The most common reason we have been given is that people feel awkward in raising these questions. There is a fear that raising these questions could be seen as being 'unprofessional'.

We would see other behaviours as much more unprofessional. Producing a proposal which is costed at ten times the prospective client's expectations is highly unprofessional. Wasting a week producing a proposal which has no earthly chance of being successful we also believe is unprofessional. Responding to the prospective client so quickly that the client uses the proposal as a basis of discussion with other providers again is unprofessional. All of these scenarios are easily avoided if the 'Commercial' funnels are explored.

The word 'professional' quite clearly has different connotations – depending on one's viewpoint. If one is speaking with a prospective client with a highly tuned commercial culture, the senior management may look upon a professional who fails to explore the 'Commercial' funnels as *extremely* unprofessional!

The professional who is good at exploring the 'Commercial' issues is in a good position to formulate a plan or strategy to win the client. In Section 5, 'Strategies Which Win New Clients', the value of this line of questioning will become even more evident.

What can be unprofessional is asking these questions in such a way that the client is made to feel uncomfortable or guarded in her response. In this section we will look not only at the questions but also how they may be phrased.

1. The Basis of Decision (BOD)

Professional   'It is quite clear to me that your company is very firm in its decision to review the whole aspect of Duty and how you can minimise its effect on your business. As you said yourself, this is something you have neither the time nor expertise to tackle with internal resources. Can I ask you, in coming to a decision as to who you will use, what will be the most important factors the organisation will consider?'

What the professional is aiming to do with this question is to open up, explicitly, the Basis of Decision (BOD) issue. Too often professionals guess at what is important to the client when she is making her decision. They try to read into the gist of the conversation what is important. Sometimes they are right and sometimes they are wrong. The professional who has explored the BOD funnel *knows*.

At times the prospective client can come back with a generic non-answer. We have to be ready for these.

Client   We want someone who is responsive, offers us good service, has people we can work with and of course is competitive fee-wise.

This is a classic non-answer. At this stage the professional has to put his listening and questioning skills to use and unbundle this. This is the skill we referred to earlier in this chapter in the section entitled 'Demonstrating our Listening'.

Professional   I'm anxious that we can demonstrate all of these attributes to you. When you say 'responsive', what exactly are you looking for and how would you like us to be able to demonstrate this to you?

This is the beginning of another funnel. Funnels exploring 'good service' and 'people we can work with' will also need to be opened, not to mention the question of 'competitive fee-wise'.

The BOD question can be explored in other dimensions. The question at the beginning of this section was phrased in such a way as to explore the organisation's Basis of Decision. This may be subtly different from the individual's Basis of Decision. The experienced professional, knowing that decisions are made and influenced by people, not organisations, will also explore this angle.

At the end of the funnels to unbundle what has previously been said, the professional may also ask:

Professional	Thank you for that. What about you? Are there any particular aspects that you personally will be looking for, from the people who help you with this?

Who knows what might come back? It could be:

Client	I'd like someone who will keep me advised of recommendations as they are forming. I personally need to be ahead of the game here. If the final conclusions are issued to all at the same time, there may be the odd person who will want to use the conclusions to their own end. I don't want to manipulate the conclusions, I just want to be sure that no one else is able to try that. I trust this is strictly off the record?

Valuable. One big step up for the professional who knows. A big disadvantage to the competing professional who does not know.

Professional	You also mentioned that your Chairman has been involved in the thinking behind this project. What things do you believe he will be looking for from the people who are selected to work on this?

Another dimension to the BOD question.

2. The monetary or budgetary issues

(Un)professional	How big is your budget?

Professionals tell us all the time that this is the question they really find difficult to ask. At the same time they also tell us stories of clients whose faces showed horror when they reached the page of the proposal on which the fees were outlined. They tell us of £35,000 proposals where the client had an expectation of 'two, maybe three thousand pounds'. They tell us of proposals where every effort was made to produce a lean and mean solution with fees to match – only to find out later that a competitor offering a much bigger and more expensive solution won easily.

We won't always get the information but the only 'crime' is not to try.

Professional	We could approach this project in a number of ways. For instance . . . . One key factor which will determine the way we formulate the final proposal will be determined by the budget you have allocated to this project. Could you give me an indication of the figure(s) you had in mind?

In this example the professional has opened up the subject by giving a good reason why the information may be valuable to the prospective client. Different ways of approaching solutions clearly have different cost implications.

Another way of introducing the subject could be:

Professional   With projects like this, when clients require outside assistance we find that some clients have a fixed and determined budget for the work whilst at the other end of the spectrum some clients find the money as and when. How does it work in your organisation?

Some prospective clients do not have allocated budgets for professional advice. Asking them directly about their budget could be a source of embarrassment and a very good reason why we sometimes get answers like, 'That's for me to know and you to find out.'

A way of raising the subject that some of us use is to smile broadly and say:

Professional   I know you'd think me unprofessional if I didn't ask – so I will. What sort of investment do you have in mind for this work?

It is the broad smile that makes the question acceptable.

It must be remembered that these examples are just funnel openers. The professional must listen to the answers and question further.

Other subsidiary questions which may occur further down the funnel are:

- What does the budget include and exclude?
- What other budgets could be utilised?
- How flexible is the budget?
- Who is the budget-holder?
- What are the sign-off thresholds?
- When does the budgetary period begin and end?
- What would happen if some more monies had to be found?

The professional in possession of this information is far better placed than his polite counterpart who thought these subjects too sensitive to raise.

3. The competitive situation

Professional   You're talking with us today about this – it's an opportunity which we appreciate. Can I ask: what other alternatives are you considering in order to resolve this issue?

Al Ries and Jack Trout, the authors of such authoritative works as *Marketing Warfare* and *Positioning*, argue that the most important issue in the sales and marketing mix is your position in relation to your competitors. Of the three 'C' elements, namely Customers, Corporation and Competitors, they state that the most important of these is your competitors – more important even than your customers.

We don't want to enter that debate here, but most times we will not be working in a vacuum. There will be other competitors and alternative solutions to ours. We have to position our final proposal to be better than the others. If we do not know what those other alternatives are, then how do we best position ourselves?

Note the question the professional has posed. He has not asked, 'Who are our competitors?'. He has asked about the 'other alternatives' which may be considered.

The prospective client may reply:

Client   Well, as you'd expect, we are talking to a couple of other people like yourselves, but there is also a possibility that we may use some internal people for this. It's another option.

The professional needs to open up the funnels indicated by the prospect with questions such as:

Professional   What would cause you to decide to use your own resources?

Professional   You said that you would be talking with others. This makes eminent sense. May I be so bold as to ask who else you will be talking to?

We will not always get the response we want to this question. Clients have said to us in the past, 'I won't tell you who they are and I won't tell them that I am talking to you.' However, far more people have told us, 'I don't mind you knowing at all. We've already seen . . . and we plan to talk to . . .'

Knowing who we are up against helps us in the way we will formulate our arguments and ultimate proposal. We will definitely put a different slant on our proposal if we are competing against a niche player compared to a mainstream competitor. Sometimes asking the 'alternatives' question can give us insight into how serious the prospective client is about seeking help. Someone who is talking to a dozen different providers may well be trawling the market for free information. In this case an early response via a proposal would be wholly inappropriate.

We have heard the argument:

'If I ask the client who they are also talking with, it may put the idea in their minds that they should be talking to other providers. They might not have thought of that.'

This is the ultimate insult to a client's intelligence. Clients buy products and services on a daily basis. Their businesses survive on the difference between the selling price of their products and services and the costs they have to meet. If a client is going to talk to three alternative providers she will already have thought of this. On the other hand if the client is convinced she wants to talk only with the people she believes to be best placed to carry out the work, she will pursue this course of action.

There is no danger in asking the 'alternatives' question. The only danger lies in ignorance.

4. The timescales

This is a fundamental funnel to explore if we are to formulate a meaningful strategy to win the prospective client's work. The following is an oft-repeated scene from the offices of one of our previous employers.

The time is 4.30 p.m. and a rather new, inexperienced consultant rushes into the building. He drops his briefcase by his desk and approaches his secretary – a very experienced lady with an in-depth understanding of the business. He has a wad of paper in his hand.

Consultant	Can you work late tonight?
Secretary	Why?
Consultant	I promised the prospect I saw this morning that we'd have this proposal on his desk by tomorrow.
Secretary	Oh? When will he make the decision?
Consultant	Look. I've promised him it will be there.
Secretary	So when will he make the decision?
Consultant	We have to be able to show that we are responsive. A proposal on his desk tomorrow will create the right impression.
Secretary	OK. Perhaps. So when is he going to make the decision?

At some point the penny drops. With some consultants who believed that no secretary could ever know more than they, the penny only dropped when they realised that they had a large number of proposals sitting on prospective clients' desks and these clients were strangely unavailable to take a telephone call.

We find that the rush to go into writing is often generated by the professional rather than the prospective client. The rather flawed thinking behind this goes somewhat as follows:

> Before a client makes a decision she must have something in writing – outlining exactly what she will get and what she will be paying. (Fair assumption.) Therefore the quicker I can get something in writing to the client, the quicker she can make the decision. (How naive!)

The professional who falls into this trap is concerned only with his *selling process*. He is totally unaware of the prospective client's *buying process*. He may be unaware that the prospect has not even engaged in a buying process.

A colleague from the past used to illustrate this phenomenon in the following words:

> 'And the creaking noise that emanated from the North that evening was another Scandinavian forest being felled to produce proposals written on the back of one-hour meetings.'

The premature proposal is a Godsend to competitors. On the assumption that a buying decision will be reached, the experienced professional, knowing the timescales, will be using this time to further his case. He will also be using the time to alter the frames of reference for the work – to his own advantage.

'Mr Efficient' who sent his proposal in the day after the meeting has a submission which is gathering dust as it is being made redundant. This is a subject we will return to in Section 5, 'Strategies Which Win New Clients'.

There are three dimensions to the timescales funnel and we would suggest that in most cases they should be addressed in the following order.

- When do you want the outputs from this project to be producing results for you?
- When do you therefore envisage that the project should begin?
- When therefore have you decided to reach a decision as to which route you will pursue for this project?

Professionals tell us constantly of clients who take ages to make up their minds and then expect that the work can start tomorrow and produce results the day after. They also tell us that they did not bring up the 'timescales' questions.

Many times clients have not thought through the time question in any detail. By asking the three questions above in the suggested order one can sometimes enable the client to realise she has an imminent decision to make.

5. The Decision-Making Process (DMP)

The scene is a training course, the subject is the Decision-Making Process.

Participant   People lie about this.

Trainer   Sorry?

Participant   They never tell you the truth when you ask them.

Trainer   What exactly are you asking them?

Participant   About who makes the final decision of course. People always lie. They always say, 'It's me.' You find out later they were lying but it's too late by then. It's not worth asking the question. I don't bother now.

The participant is right. It is definitely not worth asking that question – particularly in that way.

Trainer   Why do you want to know who makes the final decision?

Participant   (Beginning to question the course leader's 'street cred'.) That's obvious. That's who you need to be selling to.

The proposition was that we should sell to the MAN – the person with the Money, Authority and Need. This line of thinking originates from early writing on sales technique. There is an assumption that this is one and the same person – very often incorrect. There is a further assumption that the MAN will be accessible during the selling process. The real world is not always so kind to us.

What we need to find out is the *process* which the organisation will go through before a decision is reached.

We may phrase the question something like:

Professional   You've told me that you need to make a decision before the end of next month if this is going to meet the implementation dates you have in mind. Can I ask you: what will be the processes which will happen within the organisation between today and the 30th April in order that the decision is finally reached?

This is the beginning of what may be a quite extensive funnel.

Sub-questions which may suggest themselves could be:

- Who will become involved in this process?
- At what stage will they become involved?
- What will their function be in the process?
- What will their BOD be?

We have found that by trying to understand the full Decision-Making Process, it often becomes evident who makes the final decision. Whether and how they can be reached is another question.

By following the full Decision-Making Process (DMP) funnel we begin to understand the organisation to whom we are selling. By defining the process we can begin to consider our appropriate approach and strategy. Many clients will not have thought through what the process will be. This should not be unexpected. This is not like placing an order for business stationery. Most clients do not decide to employ professional advisers on a daily basis. The last time they went about it may have no relevance to how they will do it this time.

The professional who enters the DMP funnel with the 'unprepared' client can discover with this client what needs to happen in order to select an appropriate provider. The professional who fails to raise the question trusts to luck and hopes for competitors as 'gentlemanly' as he.

CHOOSING QUESTIONS FOR AN EFFECTIVE FUNNEL PROCESS

The 'Sweep-up' question

The 'Sweep-up' is used when we believe we have explored every funnel. It is usually phrased as a closed question. There are many ways of expressing the question. One way could be:

Professional   You have given me a good overall picture of the organisation and the potential significance of the Duty issue on your future decisions. We've also explored in some depth the type of assistance you require and what will be important to you. Is there anything else which you think it would be helpful for me to know?

Figure 7.5: Planning the subjects to explore

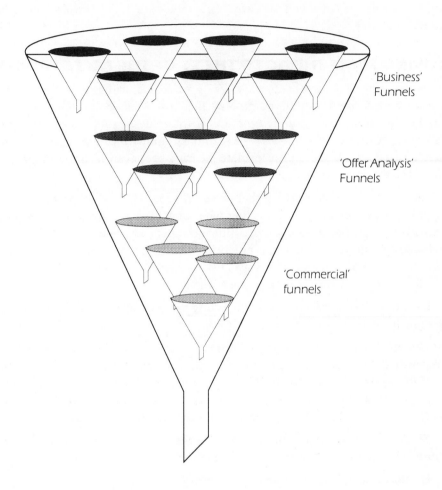

The question may or may not bring new information. The professional should be pleased if nothing more emerges. This demonstrates the thoroughness with which he has conducted what has gone before.

There is no risk in asking the 'Sweep-up' question – only potential gains. The only risk is in not asking. The question should therefore be asked in every information-gathering meeting. If there is more information, the client's response should be funnelled. Continue asking the question, perhaps phrased differently until the client says, 'No, I think that's everything.'

However, we have seen and heard professionals use the 'Sweep-up' quite early in a meeting, as soon as they have surfaced what they believe is one potential issue with a client.

Professional   That's interesting. Apart from that, is there anything else?

This repetitive and obvious technique is used for the rest of the meeting. This may suffice in a role-play in which the client is generous and 'nice'. It will not pass muster in a real meeting.

MOVING FROM THE AC TO THE ES OF THE PACES PROCESS

This is the time for a major summary. The professional will be in possession of a lot of well-won information at this point. Now the most salient points have to be brought together to form a well-rounded picture of the issues, problems or opportunities which the prospective client faces. The summary is not a boring repetition of what the client has just said. It should encapsulate the key issues in an accurate and interesting 'picture of the situation as I see it, Ms Client'.

One of the benefits of doing this is that sometimes in the course of summarising in this way, the professional can pull together what may have previously been seen by the client as disparate issues – and make connections between them. The professional can bring clarity. The professional may also bring new insight to the client. The client may begin to see the picture in a new way. This is a demonstration of expertise – helping to build an image of competence in the client's eye.

At the end of this summary it is worth asking the 'Sweep-up' one more time in case anything has been missed.

In any initial meeting the aim is to progress as far through this process as possible. When we have asked professionals how long prospective clients normally put aside for an initial exploratory meeting the answer we most often receive is, '45 minutes to an hour'. There are exceptions. If one comes highly recommended to the prospective client it is less of a risk to the prospect to give an hour and a half or even two hours.

Working on the assumption that we have checked with the prospect and we have an hour for the meeting, we need to leave ourselves ten to fifteen minutes to:

   E xplore and explain a suitable way forward.

   S eek commitment to the suggested way forward.

This means that the questioning and active listening phase of the meeting has to be completed in 35 to 40 minutes – assuming five minutes or a little more to get the meeting under way.

How can we ensure that we reach a point where, after 40 minutes, we have something to work on, something to explore further with the client, something which the client sees as an issue important enough to dedicate further time to?

Firstly, follow the structure. It works. Secondly, practise. The professional who practises more often will develop a better feel for when he needs to pursue a funnel further. He will realise more quickly when he is obtaining information for the sake of collecting information. He will learn to summarise quickly and move the discussion forward.

There are times when it is impossible to explore all of the 'Business', 'Offer Analysis' and 'Commercial' funnels in one meeting. In this case the professional will know exactly what has been explored and what remains to be examined.

Chapter 8 PAc**ES**:
Gaining Commitment

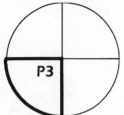

Explain or Explore a Suitable Way Forward
Seek Commitment to the Suggested Way Forward

INTRODUCTION

Closing the sale

Over the years we have had many requests to 'train my people how to close the sale. They're good with their clients but they just don't seem to be able to ask the killing question.' This request invariably comes from an individual who either does not understand the selling and buying processes or has never taken the time to observe what *really* happens when his people are in front of clients and prospective clients – or both!

Most selling is not about slick 'tricks' or 'closing techniques'which somehow get the client to say 'Yes' (against her better judgement). Selling professional services to prospective clients is particularly unsuited to any practices which have any taint of trickery about them. In most instances when a client decides to use a professional for the first time, the client is intensely aware that this is a potential on-going relationship which is being entered into. The client knows that she will have to work with these people – and perhaps have to work closely with them.

To compare this to a potential marriage may be overstating the situation to some extent. However, the analogy is not wholly inappropriate. Marriage normally occurs after a period of courtship – a period of 'getting to know you'. The prospective client is not being coy with the intent of wanting to appear virtuous or hard to get. The prospect genuinely needs to make the right choice. The wrong choice has potentially disastrous implications.

Focusing on the right process

Many professionals we work with for the first time want hints and tips which will enable them to win new clients more quickly. They want to run a more effective selling process. This focus is understandable. It is also mostly wrong. Such a focus is more likely to turn prospective clients away because the behaviours which indicate this hurried way of thinking will make themselves manifest to the prospect. To quote Maister again: 'My impressions and perceptions are created by small actions that are meaningful for their symbolism . . .'

Radical as the advice may seem initially, we recommend that professionals should forget about their focus on their selling process. Instead they should try to ascertain and understand the prospective client's likely *buying process* – and use this as the basic framework for developing the relationship.

If we pause for a minute let us consider a business that typically takes six months to a year to make a significant commitment to a new supplier. Why should Tricky John who has just been on the latest course on closing the sale succeed in one meeting? Is there likely to be such a magic formula which has somehow eluded us for the whole of our professional lives?

The professional needs to understand from an early stage the processes which the prospective client is likely to go through when appointing a new provider.

This is one purpose of opening the 'Commercial' funnels related to the Decision Making Process, the Basis of Decision and the timescales involved.

Even when our first meeting puts us in front of a decisive individual, this person alone may not make the decision for the organisation. There will usually be other decision influencers up and down the organisation who will need to be involved.

It could be argued that if we are dealing with the MAN (the person with the Money, Need and Authority – and the will to appoint us) why would we want to get involved with other people who only have influence? After all, some of that influence could be negative to our approach.

The answer is simple. If there are people who could be negative to our appointment, it is usually better to meet with them before the appointment is made. If they are presented with a *fait accompli* and feel they have not been consulted on a subject on which they have meaningful input, they may become sleeping insurrectionists – people who stealthily sabotage the work we carry out in the assignment.

The right level of commitment

All of the above does not mean that we should do our best and just wait for the client to decide when the time is right. We should maintain the initiative and work towards the highest possible level of client commitment at each stage. As the process progresses we can build that commitment at the right speed for the client – no faster and no slower.

The conclusion is that we must seek a commitment at the end of our initial meeting which the prospective client will be comfortable with. From our perspective, we must seek real commitment from the prospect. At first glance these two objectives may seem to conflict. They don't.

If, for instance, the professional seeks the following commitment at the end of the meeting there may be a problem:

Professional   Well, from our discussion you have an on-going need for legal representation on litigation issues. This product liability suit, whilst obviously a big concern for yourselves, provides us with an ideal opportunity. I would propose that you appoint us to represent you on this case. As I have outlined over the last few minutes, we have the experience and expertise to handle this. This really is our cup of tea. Could we handle this case for you?

On the assumption that the prospective client already has a firm (or a number of firms) in which it has faith to carry out the discussed case, the new provider is asking for too much. An hour after walking in off the street the eager professional is certainly asking for a commitment – but the feeling of the prospective client will be one of uncertainty and probably discomfort.

A very typical client response to such a 'close', could be:

Client   Well we intend to talk to a couple of people whom we have worked with in the past on cases like this. I tell you what, why don't you send me a proposal?

We're back to the possibility of Scandinavian forests being felled again.

The professional who responds in the affirmative to this request is in the situation of carrying through a next stage with which the prospective client is comfortable – but which demonstrates no commitment from the client.

So what is commitment? The 'golden rule' on commitment is that:

Commitment involves the prospective client in action.

In other words commitment is about getting the prospect to become involved in a buying process – but involved at a level and a pace with which they are comfortable.

EXPLAIN OR EXPLORE A WAY FORWARD

Toward the end of the questioning phase and at the point where the professional is summarising the whole picture, the brain really has to go into overdrive. At this stage the professional also needs to be concluding what commitment he will try to seek from the prospect and what he will need to say to convince the prospect to give this commitment. Not surprisingly, we have observed that listening skill is usually at its nadir at this point in the meeting. The brain cannot cope very well with the conflicting demands being made upon it.

One question which needs to be answered concerns how we position the way forward. Do we follow the advice of some and offer the prospective client a choice of ways forward (the *exploration* method) or do we simply give what we believe is the best way ahead (the *explain* approach)? There are advocates for both approaches. The supporters of the first approach are firmly convinced that most people prefer to have considered a number of options before they make up their minds with regard to any significant decision. The proponents of the second approach argue that if the professional is the expert on the subject and has previous experience then he, as the specialist, should advise the client as to the best next step. Choices would only serve to offer second-best alternatives.

The correct answer to the question is that both camps are right – depending on the circumstances. The only wrong answer comes from the person who takes a dogmatic view and insists that he follows the one route every time.

This is where the professional has to demonstrate flexibility. The best road forward will be determined by two main factors:

1. *The professional's previous track record of the problem, opportunity or issue faced by the prospect.*

    The more experience the professional has, the more likely he will be able to give advice as to *the* best next step. If a professional has extensive experience he is also more likely to sound convincing as he outlines the best way forward.

2. *The likely response of the client to being offered alternatives or just 'one best way' forward.*

    If during the meeting the prospective client utters words like 'We're looking for someone to tell us what to do', this is a different message from 'I'm looking at this problem and trying to find alternative ways we can deal with it.'

    In the first example the prospect is unlikely to warm to the professional who gives four choices. She wants to know the best suggestion from the expert. Equally, an approach aimed at convincing the client there is only one suitable way ahead will not be well received in the second example.

So, having summarised the prospect's overall position, how could the meeting go from there?

Example

Professional	Does that about encapsulate the issue you face and position it correctly?
Client	Yes, I think you have a good understanding.
Professional	OK, Jill, I know we can help you here and we would be very interested to do so. What I would like to do for a few minutes is to tell you about how we have helped other clients in a similar position and the benefits we have brought to them. Then I'd like to explore a couple of different ways that we can take this forward and agree with you the next step you'd like us to take. Is that OK?
Client	Sure. I'm waiting to hear what you think.

The professional is positive and assertive. '. . . I know we can help you here . . .'

He tells the prospective client he wants their business. '. . . we would be very interested . . .'

This is not the time to be hesitant and uncertain. People are not likely to take advice from those who are unsure. However, he has picked up the signs that this client does not want to be presented with one solution. He knows that offering alternatives does not have to be a sign of uncertainty. This is conveyed in the manner of the delivery of the message.

He is also sensitive to the fact that any next step has to be a joint agreement. A successful conclusion to the meeting cannot be the imposition of one party's preferred way forward.

Professional   As I said, the situation you have described has a number of elements which are common to other successful projects we've been involved in. How we've been able to help clients in the past is by . . .

At this point the professional has to give enough information to establish that he and his organisation have the expertise and track record to be considered potential candidates for the work which needs to be done. Expertise and track record are two elements of demonstrating competence – one of the essentials for beginning to build trust.

After a few minutes of demonstrating competence in this way, we pick up the meeting again.

Professional   . . . In summary I am certain we could do this work for you. Let me give you a couple of ways in which we could take this forward.

One alternative we could follow would be for me to meet with all of the people who have a major input into this issue. The purpose of these meetings would be twofold. Firstly I would seek their views and their concerns; and secondly, on the basis of their inputs I would put together a short presentation. I would then deliver this to all concerned – probably within a week of my final meeting. This presentation would be aimed at presenting you with a short list of the potential methods the business could adopt in dealing with the problem – and giving their likely impact in respect of your particular organisation.

The benefit of this approach is that it will get you to the point of having all of your people involved and consulted and all knowing the possible avenues which exist in order to resolve the issue.

To do this I will need you to set up meetings with a number of the people you have mentioned during the meeting. I will need to spend time with the financial director and the financial controller. In addition your head of purchasing and your marketing director should also be included as they have an interest at either end of the chain. You may suggest one or two others but I believe these four are essential. In order that the presentation fits with all concerned, we will also need to agree a date for this.

If you're able to put these meetings in place then I am very happy to make the necessary investment of my time.

Alternatively, we are running a half-day workshop on this very subject in a month's time. At this seminar we introduce specific case studies of clients for whom we have worked – helping them to resolve the kind of problems you're facing.

> It's rather easy for me to tell you in a space of five minutes that we are well equipped to handle this sort of thing but perhaps you would like to hear more of how we go about it and have the opportunity of speaking with some of our existing clients. I would be very happy for you to attend as my guest on the day and to meet with you shortly after the workshop to discuss your situation again – once you have a closer feel of how we tackle this type of assignment.

Some people we have worked with would take issue with the two alternatives suggested above. Their bone of contention goes something like this:

> Well all this person is doing is giving things away. In one instance he's giving away his professional time and in the second he is giving away a free place on a seminar. Anyone can give stuff away. We've got to be able to sell these things. They have value and the client should pay.

A very macho approach . . . and also a very unsuccessful one.

David Maister, in his article, 'How Clients Choose' has some words on this topic:

> Maybe I'll agree to meet one of your specialist partners, or consent to provide additional information to you, or provide access to one of my other executives. Perhaps I'll participate in one of your seminars or agree an additional, more focused meeting. Any one of these things should be taken as a success. If you try to rush me, I'll take it as a sign that you're more interested in making a sale than helping me.

In the example we have used, the professional has asked for specific commitments in both alternatives.

In the first case he has asked for the time of a number of senior executives – firstly in a one-on-one situation and then all together. Perhaps more significantly he has asked his client contact to 'risk' her credibility by putting him in front of some significant players from within the business. He has asked for a lot.

In the second case he has asked a senior person within the business to give up a half a day of her time to learn more about his firm. Yes, she should benefit from the experience – but she will have to give up the time. The professional has already stated that a follow-up meeting is a further commitment he will also be seeking.

Potential ways forward

There are many ways in which the professional could seek to take the dialogue further forward. Some of these options include:

* Agreement to a meeting or presentation at our offices.

* Agreement that the prospective client will prepare and send a specification for the task/project discussed.

* Agreement to a further meeting – with the prospective client responsible for inviting other interested parties.

- Agreement that the person we have met will effect an introduction to a more relevant contact within the organisation.

- Agreement that the prospect will arrange a series of one-to-one meetings in order that the project can be better understood and scoped.

- Agreement to our returning to present a discussion document to all concerned.

Seek commitment to the suggested way forward

This must be the most over-hyped subject in selling. In the Tricky John sales training course one learns 25 (or some equally ridiculous number of) ways to close the sale and get the unwilling client to say, 'Yes'. This is bunkum.

In our scenario the prospective client has now spent 55 minutes of a one-hour meeting weighing up this professional seated across from her. Take it as read – she will already have decided if she wants the dialogue to go further. She will already have come to her conclusions in respect of *credibility, competence* and *compatibility*. No trick in the last five minutes is going to change anything at all. In fact any attempt will simply backfire and damage the professional's credibility.

Avoid the temptations to try the seemingly plausible techniques such as the 'Half Nelson' which goes something like this:

Client   What you've told me is interesting and something we may have to examine further. Do you ever carry out this work in out-of-hours situations – say after 5.00 p.m. or at weekends?

Professional   If we could do that would you agree to go ahead and give us the contract?

Yuk!!

If the professional has followed the PACES process then he will not have to be concerned with 'closing'. In this case:

- He will have prepared carefully and in detail.

- He will have made a positive first impression.

- He will have positioned himself and his organisation clearly and coherently.

- He will have made it clear that he wants to understand the client's position.

- He will have explored the client's situation and requirements in detail using thought-through questions.

- He will have demonstrated real understanding through active listening.

- He will have encapsulated the whole picture in one final summary.

- He will have succinctly presented why his firm is capable of working with the prospective client.

- He will have put forward one or two logical and convincing alternatives for the way ahead.

The way ahead will be obvious to both parties. The client will usually volunteer the commitment.

If, on the other hand, the PACES process has largely been ignored for a more 'free-flowing and adaptable' (read unplanned, unprepared, unstructured and unprofessional) approach, then no super close is going to make the slightest difference.

What about the meetings which fall somewhere in between? There may be times when it is not clear if we have the prospective client's commitment. Then we have to ask.

Forget the other 23 methods. There are two which are common sense, acceptable and professional.

One is called the basic close. With the basic close the professional is simply asking the prospective client a straight question.

It may go something as follows:

Professional   . . . So, based on our experience, that would be the best way to deal with this, and the round table discussion with your technical people should be the next step.

                    Can we organise this for some time in the next two weeks?

The question requires a simple answer. If it gets a 'Yes' then all is fine; if it gets a less than total acceptance then there is some resistance which needs to be understood and dealt with.

The other acceptable way of asking for commitment is the alternative close. This is suited to the situations where we may have put a couple of suggested ways forward to the prospective client.

For example:

Professional   . . . So we could go forward either way. We can go down the route of meeting with your people and then putting together a presentation or you can come along to our seminar and we can meet again after that.

                    Which would you prefer?

Again the client is asked a simple question. This time she has two alternatives to choose from. Again, there could potentially be hesitation with both of these. The likelihood of this is in inverse proportion to the quality of the rest of the meeting which has preceded this point.

We have yet to meet the person who is genuinely competent in carrying through selling meetings with clients and prospective clients but whose sole shortcoming is that he can't close and ask for commitment. Our bet is that we will never meet that person.

Handling resistance

Professional   . . . So, in summary I believe that the way forward would be for you and your two co-directors to attend one of our half-day focus group workshops. This would not only give you some specific ideas as to how we can help but will also allow you to get a feel for our professionalism and the chemistry between our organisation and yours.

Shall I reserve you a place on our workshop on the 12th or do you think it would be more suitable next month on the 15th?

Client   I'm not sure that that would be appropriate. It seems to me that we may be rushing things somewhat.

Professional   OK. If you want to do this later on, that is no problem. As I said earlier we run these focus group workshops on a regular basis – every month in fact with the exception of August and December. Perhaps you would like to attend one of our early Autumn workshops?

Client   Possibly . . . I'll have to think about it.

Professional   Sure. Is there any other information I can give you before I leave?

Client   No, I don't think so. It's been an interesting meeting. Thanks for coming along.

Five minutes later the professional is sitting in his car. He is going back over the meeting in his mind. The opening was punchy and professional. He had spent time understanding the prospective client's situation and requirements. Some real needs which his firm could address had emerged. The client had acknowledged that these issues needed to be addressed and that they were willing to invest money in a solution. He had established that the decision would be made by joint agreement between the three executive directors and they were not talking to anyone else right now. A couple of potential competitors had already been ruled out by the client. It had all looked so promising!

But it had all gone wrong at the end. He had suggested a logical first step, quite a small initial step, the sort of first step that most prospective clients would easily say 'Yes' to. He had sought commitment – and had received a rejection. He had tried hard to retrieve the situation but had left with the, 'I'll think about it' words ringing in his ear. What had gone wrong?

On the basis that the professional's diagnosis that the P, A and C of the PACES process was right, the problems must have occurred somewhere in the E and S.

Let us look at an alternative way he may have managed the closing section of this meeting.

Professional   . . . So, in summary I believe that the way forward would be for you and your two co-directors to attend one of our half-day focus group workshops. This would not only give you some specific ideas as to how we can help but will also allow you to get a feel for our professionalism and the chemistry between our organisation and yours.

Shall I reserve you a place on our workshop on the 12th or do you think it would be more suitable next month on the 15th?

Client	I'm not sure that that would be appropriate. It seems to me that we may be rushing things somewhat.
Professional	(Pauses – waiting for prospective client to continue and expand on what she has said.)
Client	I would need to discuss this with my co-directors.
Professional	What parts exactly would you need to discuss?
Client	Well it's the whole thing about the three of us coming along to one of these workshops.
Professional	Is there some specific problem with that idea?
Client	Well, George our Technical Director has a real concern with these types of events. It goes back to a similar thing he was invited to a couple of years ago. The discussions on the workshop were meant to be totally confidential but he found out otherwise some time later. Beyond that I really don't want to go into the details of what happened but I know that he will not attend and I believe he will try to discourage John and me from participating.
Professional	Correct me if I'm wrong but during our meeting I picked up the feeling that you have an issue here which you are all anxious to resolve. I also felt that you were positive to the outline I gave of how we could help. However, the way ahead I have suggested seems inappropriate. Have I got that right?
Client	You're absolutely spot on. We do want to move forward on this but if attending a focus group workshop is the only way ahead we have a problem of acceptance.
Professional	OK, I'm sure we can sort out that problem, but let me ask: are there any other issues which would stop us taking a next step together – providing of course that the next step is acceptable to you and your co-directors?
Client	Only the chemistry thing.
Professional	(Pauses – waiting for prospective client to continue and expand on what she has said.)
	The chemistry thing?
Client	Yes. Whilst I take your idea of the workshop being a good opportunity to assess the chemistry between your organisation and ours, it is our belief that what is even more important is the chemistry between the

professional who works with us and the key people in our organisation who will be involved.

For instance, I believe that you would fit very well with the type of people we are. There may be other people in your organisation who would not. If we were to invest any further time with you we would want to be assured at this point that we would be working with individuals whom we felt comfortable with. There's no point in going any further now if we find out in three months time that your best qualified person for this type of work simply doesn't fit.

Professional   So you have a concern about who we may assign to this work and you want to be assured in some way that you would be working with individuals who are a good fit for you, your co-directors and members of your organisation with whom we may become involved?

Client   That's it.

Professional   Is there anything else that may stand in the way of us taking a next step together?

Client   No. I think I've thrown enough boulders in your path. I'm not trying to be difficult but you need to be aware of where we are coming from.

Professional   I understand completely – but if I can assure you on these two points I take it that you would be open to progressing beyond this meeting?

Client   Yes, of course.

Professional   All right, let me suggest another way forward which will address both of the points you have raised. I believe that getting you involved in a facilitated meeting format such as I originally suggested is the best way forward. However, we can vary the format of this. Instead of your attending one of our external focus-group workshops we can run one for a couple of hours here on your premises, exclusively for your company. To make it flow I would suggest involving some of your more senior managers as well as your co-directors.

I have a person in mind who I believe will work extremely well in your business. He has the right background and credentials and he has the right way of thinking to work with your people. I would be happy to send you his CV but I think that in order to get the focus of our two-hour session totally right, it would be even more appropriate for Brian and me to come along and meet with you, your co-directors and the other people whom you think would give valuable input.

Just short individual meetings would be fine – 20 to 30 minutes per person. These meetings will achieve two things. Firstly this investment of time from our side will help us in tailoring the workshop session. Secondly I know that from just a short meeting your people will be convinced that Brian has a lot to offer and they will welcome further contact with him.

Now I understand your concerns I believe that this way ahead would be even better for you. What do you think?

Client　　　That's good. When would you and Brian want to come and meet us? I think it is more important to meet my co-directors and three of the senior managers than it is to spend a lot of time with me. You seem to have a good grasp of our situation and I have confidence that you wouldn't suggest this way forward unless you were convinced that it was going to work.

Professional　　　I think the sooner the better. I have a couple of alternatives the week after next but as soon as I get back to the office I'll check Brian's availability and get back to you this afternoon. How does that sound?

Client　　　Fine!

The immediately noticeable difference between these two scenarios is that the second one is far longer. This is because the professional has made every effort to understand the reasons for the prospective client's reluctance to proceed down a suggested path.

In the first scenario the professional attempts to formulate an alternative solution without knowing the problem he is trying to tackle. He immediately attempts to move into 'convince mode' when he should begin by engaging his 'listening mode'.

In the second example the professional is following a sound process. Once he hears that the client has some uncertainty about what he has suggested, he proceeds in the following way:

Step 1　　　Pause.

Step 2　　　Question, listen and summarise (funnel) to understand the issue.

Step 3　　　Ascertain if this is the only problem.

Step 4　　　If there is another issue – question, listen and summarise (funnel).

Step 5　　　Check if there are any other issues.

Step 6　　　Test. Is the client seeking solutions or will any suggestion be rejected?

Step 7　　　Provide solutions.

Step 8　　　Seek commitment.

Step 1: Pause.

By pausing and not rushing in with either a solution or a question the professional potentially achieves four things:

1.　The pause creates the effect that he is thinking about what the client has said.

2.　The pause does give genuine thinking time.

3.　The pause may well encourage the prospective client to expand upon what she has said.

4.　If the client thinks as she talks, she may even create her own solution.

Step 2: Question, listen and summarise (funnel) to understand the issue.

On the assumption that the client has not expanded upon her initial comment, or has not expanded fully, the professional then has to open up a funnel on the subject. An open general question such as, 'How do you mean?' may be appropriate to begin the exploration of the reason for resistance. As with any funnel the professional should summarise at the end to ensure that he has got a full and accurate understanding of the issue.

Step 3: Ascertain if this is the only problem.

Having defined the reason for the resistance, the temptation is to jump in straight away and provide an answer – especially if the answer seems obvious. However, there is a danger that other problems still need to be surfaced.

In fact the first hurdle brought forward by the prospective client may not be the only one. There may be connections between the varying issues which the client raises. Therefore it is important to try to get them all out on the table.

Step 4: If there is another issue – question, listen and summarise (funnel)

This is a repeat of Step 2 should a further problem appear. Again the process should finish with a summary.

Step 5: Check if there are any other issues.

This is a repeat of Step 3 – trying to dig out all of the potential issues.

Step 6: Test. Is the client seeking solutions or will any suggestion be rejected?

This is an optional step. If we are in any doubt about the real interest of the prospective client we may carry out the test step. We may also insert this step if our solutions to the issues raised are going to involve us in expending a lot of effort or time.

In the second scenario the professional chose to insert the test step with: 'I understand completely – but if I can assure you on these two points I take it that you would be open to progressing beyond this meeting?'

Step 7: Provide solutions.

In the second scenario the professional was able to provide an alternative way forward on the spot. He was even able to link the two issues in one composite solution.

In some instances it may not be possible to provide an immediate answer. The prospective client may want a technical question answered. The answer may require research. An 'off-the-cuff' glib answer may be more of a credibility destroyer than the response, 'The last thing I want is to mislead you inadvertently. I don't have the answer. I'll have to check it out and get back to you.'

Step 8: Seek commitment.

If we have provided convincing answers to the problems which the prospective client foresaw, then it is appropriate to ask for commitment.

If it is obvious that we want to understand the prospective client's concerns and we have then provided fitting solutions, commitment will often be volunteered. In the second example when the professional asked 'What do you think?' after he had suggested the alternative way forward, the client's response indicated that she was committed to the solution.

In the first scenario no amount of 'closing' would have succeeded. The professional did not understand the issues and was not able to put a viable solution forward.

MOVING BEYOND THE FIRST MEETING

Having now obtained commitment to a next step, the professional needs to map out a campaign to win the prospect and convert her organisation to client status. Some strategies are doomed to failure from the start. Others offer a far higher potential success rate.

In Section 5 we examine the strategies which win new clients.

Section 5 **Strategies Which Win New Clients**

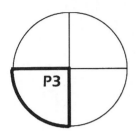

Chapter 9 **Strategies Which Win New Clients**

Introduction
Strategic Considerations
Managing the Decision-making Process
Planning and Carrying Out the Best Tactics

INTRODUCTION

We have met many professionals whose selling skills are adequate, and some whose skills are excellent, but who nevertheless achieve limited success. They tend to win small commissions from small prospects but have a poor track record in securing the big new clients which will significantly improve their business or help to make their name in the firm. These professionals often complain:

- 'It's not fair, I lost because of "politics".'
- 'They say they like our proposals but we always come second.'
- 'The clients don't seem to recognise the best solutions when they see them – we had far more to offer than the firm they chose.'
- 'She said she would have chosen us but her boss, who wasn't supposed to be involved, overrode her decision.'
- 'They are happy with their existing advisers – how can we overcome that?'

It is our experience that a major cause of these frustrations lies in the professionals' natural inclination to act rather than think; to pursue the obvious path rather than to plan the approach which *will* win the client. Excellent selling skills are not enough to win major clients. These skills must be focused in the right way, on the right people and at the right time to secure a competitive advantage which will ensure the decision goes our way.

In this section we focus on how the professional should plan his, and his firm's campaign toward each targeted prospect – how to move through the P3 section of the PACE Pipeline from a successful first meeting to create a significant new client. The ideas are not complicated. They need to be simple if they are to work in a busy world. They will however require application, motivation and *thinking* about. The time invested in productive planning and creative thinking will ensure that, when it is time for action, that action will produce results.

Nevertheless, the planning and analysis described above is only of value if it leads to *action*. Professionals whose client work demands total accuracy and comprehensive information often look for the same when planning business development. If we wait for a 100 per cent plan, we will always be too late. Often, planning descends into 'analysis paralysis' which in turn masks a reluctance to get going. To avoid this, each professional should be measured on the development of and implementation of a planned campaign. We should be questioning: Is it happening? Is it happening to time? Are the best tactics being used? Ultimately, did it succeed? It is better to proceed with a 70 per cent or 80 per cent plan which we amend as the plot develops.

Figure 9.1: Winning strategies: the whole picture

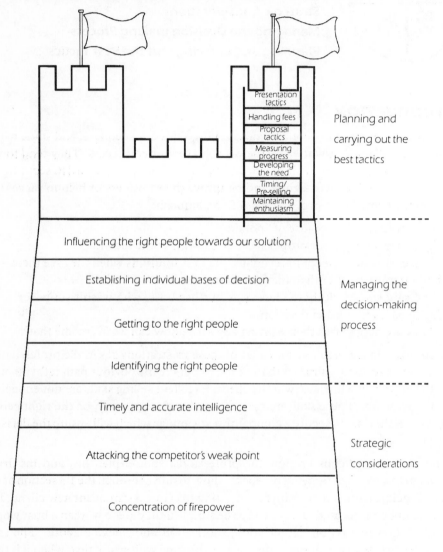

The section covers three elements:

- Strategic considerations.
- Managing the decision-making process.
- Planning and carrying out the best tactics.

STRATEGIC CONSIDERATIONS

Many textbooks draw parallels between sales and marketing strategies and military strategy. While this is sometimes taken too far we have seen that those firms who understand the principles of winning in war and can apply these principles to winning clients, have enjoyed tremendous success. We will use military analogies, sparingly, in the following discussions on how to decide the best strategy to win a significant targeted prospect.

A successful attack strategy will be based on three concepts:

- Concentration of firepower.
- Attacking the competitor where he is weakest.
- Timely, comprehensive and accurate intelligence.

Concentration of firepower

Imagine a battle in which a heavily defended fortress sits on the top of a hill surrounded by treacherous terrain for which the attacking army have no maps. This fortress is a very important prize and needs to be taken for the attackers to achieve their ultimate objective. It would be stupid of the army commander to select one soldier, arm him with a pop gun and send him off to storm the castle with the words 'Report back when you've done it!'

The soldier would feel somewhat exposed. He may try because he has been told to, he may bang his head against the brick wall several times but eventually he will give up and do something more productive. (However, the reports will probably keep coming back that: 'I'm getting there – should have some results in another day/week/month/year.')

This is exactly how a partner we know in a substantial law firm felt when he found out that he had been allocated half a dozen 'blue chip' prospects as part of the firm's 'marketing strategy'. He recognised that these prospects would make excellent clients and that his technical expertise would probably be relevant in carrying out work for them. He was also able to secure an initial meeting with a fairly senior executive at three of the six targets. However, as well as being very busy with fee-paying work, he found that, in each of the prospects where he managed to carry out a meeting, the incumbent legal advisers had a good reputation and a strong relationship. He felt at a loss as to how to proceed in his 'campaign'.

He was given the six targets because his firm was 'too reliant on existing clients' and had 'too few prospects'. This led to each partner being awarded six large prospects and told to get on with it. The firm had 120 well-defended fortresses in its sights and twenty partners with twenty pop guns and no time. Unsurprisingly none of these fortresses fell.

We have observed that the key to success is to *concentrate* effort and not spread resources too thinly even if the latter achieves the false comfort of a large prospect bank.

Figure 9.2:   Winning strategies: strategic considerations

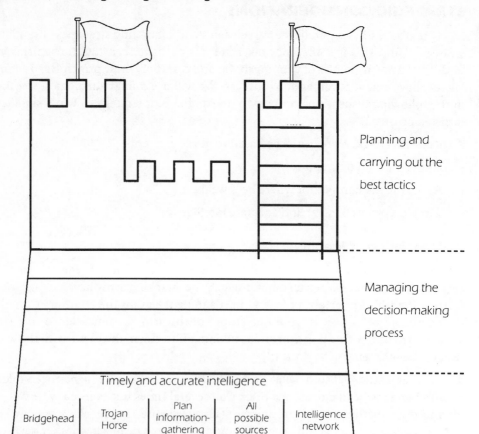

The principle of force

> Keep the forces concentrated in an overpowering mass. The fundamental idea. Always to be aimed at before all and as far as possible.

> > Karl von Clausewitz (Famous writer on military strategy)

The implication is that each of the fortresses should be attacked with *all* available firepower *one at a time*. They can be quickly overwhelmed if the attacking force is sufficiently powerful.

With regard to the law practice mentioned above this means attacking (for example) twelve prospects (not 120) with the right combination of partners and legal staff. This will help to ensure that a large proportion of those twelve become clients. This is especially important where the incumbent advisers are strong or have been in place a long time. The defenders will almost always retain control unless those looking to win the client are able to create a competitive advantage.

To create a competitive selling advantage in a professional environment, where the firm is selling its expertise and its people, requires the attacking organisation to focus the right quantity and an overwhelming quality of resource at the point in the client relationship where the incumbent competitor is weakest.

Attacking the competitor where he is weakest

> You can be sure of succeeding in your attacks if you only attack places which are undefended.
>
> Sun Tzu (Chinese Warlord)

There are at least two strategies we could choose from when attacking a new client. They are:

1. *Frontal Attack* – go in with all guns blazing and try to knock the competitors out by:

   - Having the best 'product'.
   - Having the cheapest price.
   - Being better at selling.

2. *Flanking Attack* – identify areas of weakness in the competitor's situation, service or relationship and focus all efforts on winning in that area. This establishes a bridgehead from which to compete at a later date on more advantageous terms with the incumbent.

The latter is more likely to succeed and yet the former is almost always attempted!

For example Mark, a tax specialist confronted with a situation where a prospect is spending £100,000 every year on corporate tax advice with her existing adviser, may be tempted to compete for that work. The existing adviser has a strong relationship and has provided a good service so that although Mark and his team spend considerable time and effort on meetings, proposals, presentations and negotiations to win the assignment, the prospect eventually decides to stay where she is. The incumbent has probably had to drop his rates but this is little reward for Mark.

If, in the same scenario, Mark had explored more deeply he might have found that the prospect had one small subsidiary which imported raw materials and exported finished goods around the world. He may also have found out that the incumbent advisers had limited expertise in international taxation but were excellent on domestic issues. Then, if Mark or his team had the relevant specialist knowledge and had applied all their efforts to securing that assignment, the results might well have been different.

Instead of winning nothing, Mark would probably secure one piece of work. Mark then has the opportunity to:

- Produce excellent work which puts the incumbent to shame.

- Get to know people with influence in the subsidiary and at head office.

- Be in a much better position a year later to win the major taxation work as an existing adviser with a known track record and 'allies' within the client.

So why do professional firms insist on going for a frontal attack? Usually because:

- The prize is so tempting it blinds them to any other options.

- Everybody wants quick success, which leads to more patient approaches being discarded.

- A frontal attack strategy means no thought-through strategy at all. All that happens is that when an opportunity is identified everyone leaps into action.

Another reason why 'full steam ahead' becomes the order of the day is that to identify the competitor's weak points and then to plan the best approach takes time, effort and skill in intelligence-gathering.

Timely, comprehensive and accurate intelligence

> Foreknowledge cannot be elicited from spirits; it cannot be obtained inductively from experience, nor by any deductive calculation. Knowledge of the enemy's dispositions can only be obtained from other men.

> Sun Tzu

In any war the most important commodity is intelligence. Spies (or spy satellites) produce information on the terrain, the defences and the opposition's movements. This intelligence dramatically influences a commander's choice of action. With superior intelligence one can almost always 'outwit' the opposition.

In exactly the same way if, after one meeting, we believe we know enough about a prospect to launch a successful attack we will be fooling ourselves. On our training programmes, when participants are sceptical or bemoan the time taken on information gathering we ask them to think about their own, usually large, organisation. We ask them to think what would happen if their firm was considering a purchase which was expensive, impacted on several departments and would have a considerable impact on the bottom line of the organisation. Then we ask them to think through the discussions and meetings, the 'fors and againsts', the 'politics' and the stumbling blocks which would be involved in such a purchase. We ask them to think about the people who would have a lot of influence and others who only thought they would!

Participants often describe a tortuous process – if they even know. This (less than perfect) understanding comes from 'living' in the firm for several years. How can this insight possibly be gained in one or two meetings? And yet having this insight (in effect a map of the terrain and a knowledge of the correct paths and the dead ends) is often *the* difference between success and failure.

This is one obvious reason why the incumbent, if he keeps an up-to-date knowledge of the client and any changes in people and priorities, is in a favoured position. He should know which buttons to press and whose support to enlist.

Generally after one meeting we will have managed to train a spotlight onto a small part of the organisation with the rest remaining a dark hinterland. How do we bathe the rest of the terrain in strong floodlights?

Gathering intelligence
Secure a 'bridgehead' assignment

As discussed above, secure a small assignment as a bridgehead and make sure the opportunity is used to talk to, and more importantly listen to, anybody and everybody who may have useful information.

Consider a 'Trojan Horse' strategy

A Trojan Horse strategy offers the prospect a service of value to them – at no cost. For example an accountancy firm may offer to spend a couple of days helping to train the financial controller's staff in their use of accountancy software in order to increase the efficiency of the department. This service should not be described as 'free' but as an investment of time in establishing a relationship.

The *quid pro quo* provided by the client is the opportunity for us to penetrate parts of their organisation which otherwise would be unreachable. In this example it could include accounting staff, IT staff and senior managers in other functions who receive data from – and provide data to – the finance department. If this project has value to the prospect and also enables us to shed light on the internal workings of the organisation it will generate superb intelligence upon which to plan the winning of substantial pieces of work. It may even help us to identify an opportunity for work which we never would have been able to recognise through any other process.

Plan information-gathering

Produce a thought-out, detailed plan of action which is then strictly monitored and reviewed covering:

- What information is required.
- What are the information sources.
- Who will do what to gather the information.
- When will the actions be carried out.
- How and when will the information be reported back.
- Who will assemble the information.
- What review meetings need to be in place to discuss the information gained, to plan further phases of the process and ultimately decide how to use the information to win.

Gather information from all possible sources

Published information

Published information is especially valuable in situations where the words give an insight into the culture, ethos and aims of the organisation. This might be in the form of reported interviews with the chief executive, press statements, report and accounts and company literature.

Much of this information is now easily available electronically. We should always check the existence and content of a Defined Prospect's Internet Web site.

Sources inside our own firm

Very often much of the information we need is known by a selection of people who work alongside us. Some of our colleagues may have had dealings with key people in the prospect in 'past lives'. Some may have personal friends or past colleagues working for the prospect.

Some people may know somebody who knows somebody who knows somebody. It is a crime not to tap this rich source of insight by at least making it easy for anyone to come forward and be 'drained' of all potentially useful information. In our experience, especially in large firms, this is a trick that is missed.

Last year when speaking to a group of managers from a remote regional office the subject of a high profile bid recently lost by the London practice came up. The reaction from one of the group was 'If they'd asked me I could have told them what to do – I know the chap who is the assistant to the Director who made the decision. I didn't even know they were going for that company.'

Other suppliers to the prospect

We often have contacts with people who work for complementary suppliers who have already *won* business from this prospect. How did they do it? Could this information be of use?

'White Knights' within the prospect

Most importantly we should aim to develop an intelligence network *within* the prospect organisation. The aim is to have as many people as possible in different positions who are able to provide an all-round view of the situation – almost a 3D map of the terrain. From these people we would like to know:

- Answers to all the Commercial Questions described in Chapter 7.
- The competition's strengths and weaknesses in the eyes of the decision-makers.
- Our perceived strengths and weaknesses.
- How we are doing.
- What our next steps should be and anything else which helps us on our way.

But why should somebody in the prospect organisation provide us with all of this information?

There are two reasons:

Reason 1 – someone on our side has a relationship with the person. This may have stemmed from an earlier business relationship or from contact at conferences, seminars, institution meetings etc. These relationships are the most useful because they are in place *before* the campaign to win this client begins. The information can therefore be used at an early stage of planning and can help to ensure that we follow the right track from the start. If the firm is to be in this position in as many situations as possible then:

• Everyone in the firm should be active in building potentially useful relationships with as many people working in the firm's target markets as possible. This activity, while never appearing to be urgent, is tremendously profitable in the longer term as the firm builds a network of contacts ready for 'activating' at the appropriate moment.

• The knowledge of 'who knows whom' should be assembled and co-ordinated so that it is to hand when needed.

*Reason 2 – he or she **wants us to win**.* This may stem from a relationship described above and may be in place before the start of the selling campaign. Alternatively, as the campaign progresses and we meet a number of people whom the decision will affect, we convince some of them that our approach, expertise or solution will be the one which benefits them or their department and in doing so we enlist them to our cause. We will explore this process in more detail below. It is sufficient to say that if many people want us to succeed and we make use of that motivation in a professional manner, we should have a wonderful source of accurate information about both the 'hard' facts and the 'soft' issues in the prospective client's organisation.

At this point the terrain becomes floodlit, the best paths become clear, the competitor's strengths and weaknesses are obvious and we can:

• Decide on the best strategy.

• Plan the correct tactics.

• Concentrate our firepower.

• Go on to win the prospect!

MANAGING THE DECISION-MAKING PROCESS

In a simple world the prospect's decision to purchase our services would be made by one person sifting through the facts and deciding on the best solution. In that case we would need only to identify who that person was and arrange to go and persuade her why she should choose us.

Life – and sizeable prospects – are, however, not like that. Once again we should consider how important decisions are made in *our* firm. If we think about the ebb and flow of influence, the different people involved, the people who are consulted – and those who are not – and the motivations behind each person's contribution, it becomes obvious that managing the decision-making process in a client or prospect requires a lot of thought and a planned approach.

Figure 9.3:   Winning strategies: managing the decision-making process

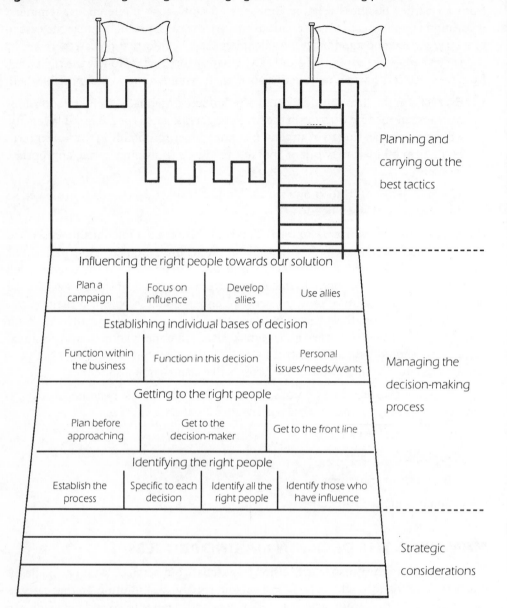

In managing the decision-making process our objective is:

**To influence all of those who will influence the decision
towards our solution.**

Ideally everyone should be influenced directly through one-to-one meetings. Once again it is clear that pursuing the 'one meeting then a proposal' strategy with prospects will not work. If we are to influence the right people we need to:

- Identify who they are.

- Get to them.

- Establish their individual bases of decision.

- Plan to influence them.

Identifying the right people

In Section 4, Chapter 7 we spent some time examining the Commercial Funnels in the funnelling process. If we are able to gain an accurate understanding of those particular funnels we will be some way towards identifying the right people. We recommend that early on, and at every stage of the sale, the prospect is encouraged to discuss in detail the *process* involved in making this decision and to identify who will be making a contribution. You will note that this does not mean asking, 'Are you the decision-maker?' This is like saying 'Do you write the cheques around here mate?' and is likely to get a defensive, inaccurate and incomplete response.

Assuming we have established a rapport, developed credibility and asked our questions in the right way we should build an accurate picture as our contacts see it. We need to know:

- Who will make the final decision.

- Who will be affected by the purchase and will be consulted in the process.

- Who has specialist knowledge and will therefore have an input.

- Who will screen out bidders at different stages of the process.

- Who may be consulted by the decision-maker and influencers although they are not specifically affected by this decision.

- Any others whose influence could sway the decision.

Several issues make this process more difficult (see Table 9.1).

Table 9.1: Identifying the right people – a potential minefield

Problem 1

Sometimes an individual says (or even believes) that she is the ultimate decision-maker but when the chips are down we find that someone else overrides the decision and decides to go with a competitor who has been selling to them.

Solution 1

By questioning carefully we must ensure that our contact doesn't feel their status is being challenged. This might lead to them overstating their authority.

Find out from other sources in the prospect their view of who the ultimate decision-maker is.

Explore the process the decision will take in order to identify any final stages which have not been explained.

Problem 2

We have experience with this client or others like them which leads to incorrect assumptions about who will be involved and their level of influence.

Solution 2

The decision-making process varies between prospects. This depends on the culture of the organisation (e.g. democratic, centralised, devolved etc.) and their past experience of this type of purchase. It may also change over time.

If last year the Managing Director was the ultimate decision-maker then this year, having had experience of purchasing this type of service, she may well devolve responsibility to the Finance Director, even if the size of the budget has increased.

Conversely, if economic conditions worsen Managing Directors start to count paperclips! In this case the responsibility for certain levels of decision-making will tend to move up the organisation.

We should never make assumptions based on past experience. We must always find out how this decision will be made and keep up to date with any changes in the process as it progresses.

We cannot assume that the ultimate decision-maker is always the most senior executive but, conversely, we should not accept that the decision rests at a lower level just because the right person (e.g. the Chief Executive) is difficult to reach. We must use our contacts in the client organisation to ensure our understanding is correct.

Problem 3

We establish the 'important' decision influencers but forget about the people who will be affected day to day such as:

- the clerks in the finance department for general accountancy work;
- the factory workers, supervisors and shift managers for a re-engineering project;
- the salespeople when discussing a training programme.

In some organisations these people will have no influence on the decision. In many others, however, their views will be canvassed. Picture the scene in a manufacturing company coming to the final decision on employing consultants to improve quality of production.

Managing Director:

'Well I think it boils down to two alternatives. They both appear fine to me. Any views Fred?'

Production Manager:

'Not really George, I think both of these outfits understand our business and have a very good track record. I did speak to the lads this morning and Joe, in the finishing shop, mentioned that the consultants from Cambridge had spent some time with him. He was impressed that they seemed down to earth and were willing to listen. I think they allayed some of his fears.'

Managing Director:

'That's useful. OK let's go with them then.'

The dialogue may seem fanciful but we have seen many important decisions turn on very small factors for and against. As companies become more democratic the people in the know (i.e. at grass roots) are likely to be consulted more and more.

Solution 3

Everyone affected by the decision must be identified and as many as possible influenced.

Even if these people are not consulted by their superiors before the decision, we may find they are lining up to sabotage our efforts if they have been convinced by one of our competitors and not by us.

We will discuss how to get to them in the next section.

Problem 4

The organisation chart can lie! People with grand, and seemingly relevant jobs and titles may turn out to have little influence. Others lower down the organisation, and perhaps to one side, end up having a major influence on how the ultimate decision-maker decides.

There is a distinction between INFLUENCE and AUTHORITY. Authority is obvious from titles and organisation charts. Influence is invisible until it has been used. We need to understand where the influence lies.

Many a contract has been lost by the selling firm identifying the wrong horse to back – the outcome is usually a cry of 'Foul' or 'It's not fair – we lost because of politics.'

Solution 4

We must know who has, and will have, INFLUENCE on this decision. In most cases this insight needs to come from people within the prospect organisation, or others who know it very well. Excellent questioning of our contacts will help.

'Who has an interest in the results of this project?'

'Who will you or the MD consult before deciding?'

'Who are the people whose views will carry greatest weight?'

The most productive source will, however, be those of our contacts who want us to win. These people can be asked even more searching questions.

'Who has X's (the decision-maker's) ear?'

'Who does X sit next to at lunch?'

'Who tends to get her way in the organisation?'

'Whose opinion will be discounted?'

'Who, in this group, is seen to be weak, out of date or out of favour?'

The answers to these questions will allow us to overlay our understanding of influence on our knowledge of the organisation structure. This will give us the real lie of the land upon which to plan the use of our resources to greatest effect.

Identifying the right people – footnote

Unless we know who the 'right' people are, all the high-powered selling resource in the world is not going to win us the client. An accurate understanding, however, will give us an excellent chance of winning. To do this we need:

- Excellent information-gathering (funnelling) skills.

- As many 'allies' as possible feeding us accurate information at the right time.

Getting to the right people

Plan your initial approach

Most of us have found ourselves in the position where we are blocked from getting to some key influencers, and very often the decision-maker herself, by the first person we contact in the prospect organisation. This may happen because he wants to 'keep control', because he overestimates his own power or because we haven't gained enough credibility for him to be comfortable in introducing us to others. Most often we will be fighting a losing battle here by relying on him to press our case or by trying to influence others at arm's length.

Many participants on our training programmes ask us for advice on how to get out of this situation.

The problem is that any course of action at this stage has risks attached – either in losing the business or in alienating our contact. The only real advice is not to get into the position in the first place!

At one level this means handling the initial meeting so well that our contact is keen to allow us to penetrate all and any parts of the organisation we want. We would do this by building credibility, by posing no threat to this person or their position and by 'selling' them on the benefits of our meeting all the key people. The skills involved in achieving this have been examined in Section 4.

At a more fundamental level should this person have been our first point of contact at all? It is easier to slide down an organisation than to climb up, so should we have gone in higher to start? With some insight into the people concerned could we have known that this person would be a 'blocker' and therefore have planned to meet them later in the process once we have built a relationship with others in the organisation?

Too often professionals get themselves in this extremely frustrating position because:

- They take the route of least resistance and 'see the people who will see them'.

- They do not gather intelligence *before* making the approach.

The route of least resistance often means:

1. Identifying a likely prospect.

2. Picking out someone whose title appears 'about right'.

3. Making contact with him in the way which feels most comfortable.

4. Taking it from there!

If the prospect is worth winning, it is worth investing time in research beforehand. Ideally we should get some insight into the decision-making process of the prospect before making the first approach. We should do this by exploiting all possible sources of information in the marketplace, our own firm and in the prospect organisation itself.

It may be time-consuming but not as time-consuming as a series of prospective client meetings which go nowhere. If our information is very limited then our guiding principle should be that the first point of contact should be higher than necessary rather than lower.

Getting to the decision-maker

While the decision-maker should not be the only focus of our activity it is critical that we get her on our side. It is risky to rely on others in her organisation to make our case for us. The decision-maker can also give us insight that others cannot.

If it is appropriate to make the decision-maker the first point of contact then first she must be identified and secondly persuaded that it is worth her while meeting with us. The tailored letters and telephone techniques described in Section 2, Chapter 4 will help us but the most powerful weapon here is the referral. If somebody whose opinion she values says: 'You really ought to see these people' or our letter refers specifically to someone she respects and then this approach is followed up correctly, it will almost certainly gain us an audience where our credibility is already high as we walk through the door.

These referrals can be gained by trawling the firm's contacts in existing clients and elsewhere and by *asking* for them. If no referrals are available in this way, and we are unable to get to the decision-maker directly, the referral source must be cultivated inside the prospect. That is, we need to develop allies of those people whose judgement she respects so that at the right time we can book a meeting on their recommendation. This in turn comes back to planning the initial approach and to understanding who has influence in the organisation. Conversely if we get it wrong and a senior colleague, whose judgement she has no regard for, says 'You really ought to see them, I think they have a lot to offer', our chances have certainly taken a step backwards.

Later on in this section we will look at how to influence the key people towards our solution. Suffice it to say at this stage that to reach the decision-maker we may need to focus our efforts on getting some key influencers to put us in front of her.

A final thought. Professionals often aim too low in the target organisation. They are more happy working with Technical Directors or perhaps Finance Directors who 'talk their language'. To sell effectively in today's environment however, the professional needs the skills and the confidence to add value to a meeting with people at every level. If we can't, and our competitors can, we will always be at a disadvantage.

Getting to the front line

In our earlier scenario, Joe from the finishing shop was instrumental in a decision which may have related to a million-pound purchase of consultancy services. That won't always be the case but an army of supporters is far better than an army supporting the opposition. Sometimes those who will be working with the results of our actions need to feel that they have been listened to.

If we show that we are listening, if we can meet them and demonstrate that we are human, practical and understand their problems and if we can start to develop a relationship with them we will be much more likely to win the business. We will also be more likely to enjoy their co-operation when doing the work later. But, if there is one decision-maker and a handful of senior influencers there may be tens or hundreds at 'lower' levels. How can we possibly get to them?

Step one   We 'sell' the idea of our meeting them to our existing contacts who are then keen for it to happen.

Step two   We decide who to see. A representative sample or a particular department may be sufficient. People in these groups will pass on the message to others. The more we want the business, the more people we will see.

Step three   We decide on the appropriate resource at every level. For example the Senior Partner for the Managing Director, other Partners for the senior executives and managers and seniors to be in contact with the front line troops.

Step four   We execute the plan. This may involve interviews, group discussions, seminars or factory visits. A Trojan Horse project may also be appropriate here.

We have now identified those people who will influence the decision. We also have plans to get in front of the right people. The next part of the jigsaw concerns how to understand the basis on which each person will influence the decision so that we can then plan to move them toward recommending us.

Establishing individual bases of decision

Our objective throughout this process is to 'influence all of those who will influence the decision towards our solution'. When we have identified the right people, and have been successful in reaching them, our next aim is to persuade each of them of the merits of our case. As discussed in Sections 3 and 4 we can only persuade someone if we understand their perceived needs, real needs and wants and the basis upon which they will make their decision.

In essence, rather than exploring and influencing one iceberg, the task now is to explore and understand a sea full of icebergs of different shapes and sizes. Just as it is inappropriate to present the same message to different clients it is also inappropriate to have one line of persuasion for each person involved in the decision-making process.

There is obviously a need for consistency of message but within that general approach each person needs to be sold to differently. For example, consider a situation with two key decision influencers where one is by nature cautious and keen for the project not to fail and the other is keen to use the most creative solution and for the project to be very high profile.

Both of these people need to be convinced. All it may require is that in discussions with the former the professional stresses his firm's track record, the number of this type of project carried out and the fail-safe mechanisms in place to make sure it is delivered successfully. These points, however, would not interest the latter person who will need to hear how 'state of the art' technology is used, how creative is the input and what impact the project will have on the business.

It is completely feasible that one project can be presented in two, or more, different ways – the key is to know what will persuade each person and then to use that insight to rally them to our cause. We need to understand in detail each person's 'iceberg'.

There are three key elements to consider for each influencer:

*   What is her function within the business?
*   What is her function in this decision?
*   What are her individual/personal issues, needs and wants?

Function within the business

The Sales Director of a company may want to know how our solution will affect his team, the competitiveness of the company's products and services and his people's ability to beat the competition to achieve 'top line' results.

The Finance Director, on the other hand, may be more interested in the effect on costs, reporting systems and the bottom line at each operating unit.

The Managing Director may be expected to take the broad view but this will depend on his own background (finance, marketing etc.) and his ambitions for the business.

Personnel Directors, Technical Directors, Production Directors, Health and Safety Managers and other managers throughout the business will all have their own 'turf' which will in turn influence their views.

Obviously the title of each person is not enough information to work on. It will be necessary to explore each person's responsibilities, the issues in their department or team and, very importantly, what they are measured on. This understanding will give us part of the story.

Function in this decision

While the influencers' input will depend in part on their responsibilities within the organisation, they may also have a specific input relating to this particular decision.

1. The decision-maker's function will be to make the final decision with more or less input from others depending on her management style and on the circumstances. If the decision-maker is responsible for the bottom line and future development

of an organisation or a business unit she will make her decision based on how each proposed solution affects the present or future success of the business.

2. One or more influencers may be responsible to the decision-maker for ensuring that all proposals are up to standard and meet whatever specifications are set down. These people need to be convinced that the bid or proposal is compliant.

3. The people in the business who will be affected day-to-day by the purchase (for example the front line troops, their managers and others in affected departments) may well be giving input into the decision.

    Their function is to consider how each solution will affect them in carrying out their work. Their advice will focus on how each proposal affects their ability to perform their tasks – in terms of speed, quality etc. They will also consider personally how it makes their jobs more interesting, productive, rewarding, safe or easy to do. As noted earlier these people tend nowadays to have more and more influence and yet are the people most frequently ignored by sellers.

The three categories described above represent the roles people play. Different people will play different roles in different decisions. It is fatal to assume that we know who will play the roles based on past experience. Each decision requires investigation to find out who will be doing what in *this* instance.

Some people may play more than one role at a time. For example the decision-maker (1) may also be affected day-to-day by the decision (3) or one of those on the front line (3) may also be given responsibility for checking compliance (2).

There may be others in the process who do not fit neatly into the categories described above. Outside consultants may have an advisory role or a general manager from an unrelated department may be asked for advice by the decision-maker because she respects his thinking. Someone else in the business may be asked to contribute because they have specific experience or specialist knowledge.

We should beware of trying to force these people into boxes. It is important to understand for each of these very influential people:

*   What their role is in this decision.

*   What they need to know to support our case.

*   How we best put information across to them in the most persuasive way.

This final question brings us to the person rather than the role.

Personal issues/needs/wants

The iceberg principle has been explained fully in Section 3. In managing the decision-making process we need to bring all of our skills to bear to gain a real insight into each person's 'iceberg'. With the opportunity to meet each of them we can question, listen and funnel to understand what makes each of them tick.

We need to know for each person their individual:

- ambitions;
- fears;
- concerns;
- prejudices;
- past experience;
- issues;
- motivations;
- relationships with others;
- views of the project, us, the competition;
- and much more.

If we are unable to meet some of the key influencers we should gain what insight we can from our allies into what makes these people tick. When we gain an accurate understanding of:

- what makes each person tick;
- what role they will play in this decision;
- what function they perform in the business;

we will be in a position to plan what to say to each of them to persuade them towards us and our solution.

Influencing the right people towards our solution

We may need to influence two or three people or, in a major opportunity, dozens. Whichever is relevant we need a campaign planned at the start of our approach and modified as our understanding of the prospect improves.

- This campaign plan should include an analysis of the decision-making process in all its facets described above.
- Based on this analysis we need to decide on who has more or less influence and who is more or less open to our ideas. This should determine the order in which we plan to see people.
- The whole campaign should be directed towards making use of any allies already in place and developing as many of the right allies as quickly as possible early in the campaign.

Who are the 'right' allies?

As we mentioned earlier we clearly do not want people vociferously supporting us who are regarded badly by their colleagues. We do however want to enlist those who have great influence in appropriately high places and who have an interest in the outcome of this decision. These are powerful allies. Ultimately the most powerful ally of all is the decision-maker. If she is keen for us to win and her trusted advisers agree, we are in the strongest possible position.

- Allies are developed by persuading them of the merits of our solution in *their* terms – personally, departmentally and in relation to their role in this decision.

  It is in this situation where professionals who are very 'technically' orientated make the mistake of presenting their solution in terms of the technical issues to everyone in the decision-making process. While this may be appropriate for those with a responsibility for screening out proposals on the basis of technical suitability it will be counter-productive for those whose interests are in either the bottom line of the business or in how it affects their day-to-day work. These people need to hear about the benefits to them of our proposals.

- It is clear that the success of the campaign relies heavily on two things:
  - The 'intelligence network' and team of allies which are in place or which can be developed.
  - Our skills at understanding, persuading and gaining credibility with different types of people with different motivations.

With the strategic plan in place the next stage will be to decide upon and implement the best tactics.

PLANNING AND CARRYING OUT THE BEST TACTICS

Introduction

The plans and strategies have been developed. Now the professional has to carry them out successfully. The focus is on winning! Coming 'second' gets no prizes. Now is the time to invest the appropriate energy and resources to make sure that we are successful. This section concentrates on how to carry them through. However, before we consider how best to manage the process, let us consider the situations where our freedom of movement is limited.

Situations where the process is dictated to us

Some of our clients tell us that they have no control over the buying process once a bid is being pursued. For example in a sizeable public sector project the client may strictly define the specification and limit the actions allowed by the selling organisation and its personnel. In these situations the winner will be the organisation which has the 'best' solution or the cheapest price or both. If the approach is totally dictated by the buying organisation there is no opportunity to 'sell'. However, we would give the following guidance.

There are only a few situations where there is no freedom of movement.
Very often we limit ourselves by not exploring and challenging the process in detail. We do not 'sell' the client on the benefits she will derive from a more flexible approach. The unpalatable truth is that if we are reliant on these very restricted situations our work will be at very low margins or even loss-making unless we are significantly more efficient than our competitors. If the margins are low then it is even more imperative for us to secure work in other buying situations where greater flexibility allows us to put forward a better case and to command reasonable rates.

Stretch the rules where possible
Where there is some flexibility we would recommend stretching the rules as far as possible without alienating any members of the decision-making process. In that case we should select some of the ideas outlined below and try them out – see how far we can go and what advantage that brings us.

Build relationships early
If our freedom of manoeuvre is limited once the bidding process starts, but the prospect has some discretion in purchasing, then our chances will depend on the relationships we have built up *before* the project becomes 'live'. This in turn depends on using the strategies and tactics descibed in this section both to get on the tender list and to give ourselves an advantage over the competition once there.

In situations where there is a flexible process, or no defined process at all, we must take advantage of the situation to ensure we win. If we have selected the right strategy, gathered intelligence, and at least started to understand the decision-making process then the following tactics will help us to move from first contact to ultimate success.

Figure 9.4: Winning strategies: planning and carrying out the best tactics

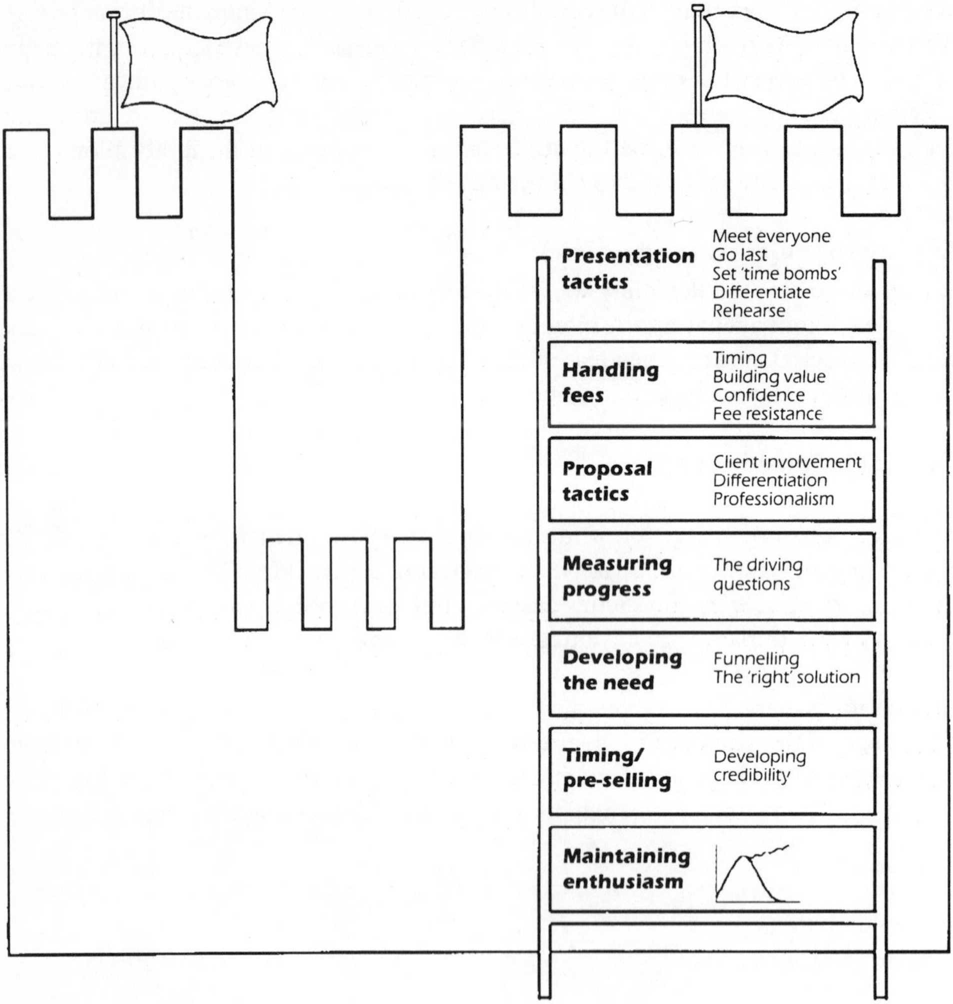

Presentation tactics	Meet everyone Go last Set 'time bombs' Differentiate Rehearse
Handling fees	Timing Building value Confidence Fee resistance
Proposal tactics	Client involvement Differentiation Professionalism
Measuring progress	The driving questions
Developing the need	Funnelling The 'right' solution
Timing/ pre-selling	Developing credibility
Maintaining enthusiasm	

Maintaining enthusiasm

Figure 9.5 represents a situation faced by many professionals.

Imagine a speculative first meeting with a prospective client. This prospect has enough interest to agree to a meeting – represented at point 1 in Figure 9.5. The meeting itself goes extremely well. We develop great rapport and compatibility, gain a high level of credibility and demonstrate competence. We also get to understand *and agree* some issues critical to the business which need to be addressed and put forward some ideas with which the prospect is highly impressed. We stay for two hours when we originally expected 40 minutes.

The prospect not only takes us back to reception but walks with us back to the car saying, 'I am very impressed. I know that you could bring added value to the

Figure 9.5:   How enthusiasm drops

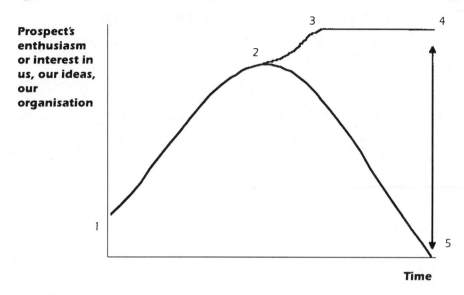

We are now at point 2.

As we float on air back to the office we think that perhaps business development is not so bad after all. We go to see the Senior Partner and describe the situation in glowing terms, in fact we probably remember an even more positive situation than we actually heard – maybe up to point 3.

We drop the prospective client a line to thank her for the meeting and wait for her to call. Eight weeks pass and we start to watch the phone. At ten weeks we are a little disappointed but she did say 'a couple of months' and these things do tend to get delayed. At twelve weeks we wonder whether to phone but we don't want to pester her. At fourteen weeks the Senior Partner is getting on our back because this organisation has been on our list of good prospects for months now. Eventually at sixteen weeks we pluck up the courage and ring her:

Professional	Good morning, Janet, it's Peter Smith from CBD.
Client	Er . . . hello.
Professional	I hope you don't mind but I was ringing to follow up our meeting in January.
Client	Umm . . . remind me.
Professional	Oh sure! We were talking about ways of providing some creative solutions to the problems you were having in France and Germany.
Client	Oh. Right. What was the name again?

Professional	Peter.
Client	Oh yes. Peter remind me, how did we leave our discussions?
Professional	You were going to phone me so that I could come in and meet the MD to discuss what we could do.
Client	I remember now. As it happens the issues in France and Germany came to a head three weeks ago. We had to get some quick solutions so Jim arranged for our existing consultants to go over and recommend some changes. They've just produced their draft report. I am still interested in talking to you when other issues arise, but it would probably not be appropriate to meet now. Look, please keep in touch, I would be interested to hear of any developments.
Professional	Oh, sure, OK.
Client	Thanks for phoning. Goodbye.

One thing is for certain here. The client's level of interest, let alone memory of the meeting, was a lot lower than the professional expected! The professional has a memory of the meeting which has not changed in the intervening weeks (now at point 4) while, for whatever reasons, the prospect's enthusiasm has reduced dramatically to point 5. Why the drop? Perhaps the story goes something like this:

- As soon as the prospect got back to her office the MD came in with a rush job to do by Monday.

- On Monday she learnt that she would have to present the findings to the world-wide board and one of her most trusted subordinates handed in his resignation.

- During the next week a fault in the computer system created havoc in her department, she learned that her best friend had had her first baby (and a letter arrived thanking her for a meeting last week).

- Over the next two weeks the firm secured a large order, decided to move to new premises and narrowly averted a strike in its Spanish factory.

- In the next month things really went mad at work, she was working 70 hours a week and, partly because of this, her husband left her for his secretary etc. etc.

In other words there have been more things on her mind than the meeting *we* remember so vividly. No wonder four months later she couldn't remember us, let alone the meeting.

The diagram should focus our minds on one simple aim – to maintain and develop the prospect's level of enthusiasm so that it is as high as possible at the right time. In this situation the professional's principal task is to ensure that the level of interest follows line (a) not line (b).

When an issue becomes current we must be right at the front of her mind and not a distant memory. How can we do this?

Figure 9.6:   Maintaining enthusiasm

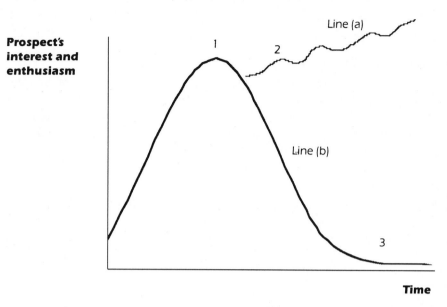

Maintain telephone contact

At the end of the meeting we could explain to her that we would like to consider the information we have gained and that if we have any further queries on the detail we may ring her in the next few days. She is enthusiastic at this stage and will always say 'Yes'. We should then ring her – even if there are no real gaps in our information – we can ask a couple of questions and take the opportunity to remind her of the things that made her enthusiastic at the meeting.

Write

We can write a letter to arrive three to four days after our phone call. This letter does not just thank her for the time, it also summarises the key issues she faces and the things she liked about how we might approach such a situation.

Meet with other people

Other interested parties may have been identified during the meeting. We should ask to see them early rather than wait for any project to be 'live'. In this way their views can be taken into account. Timing is key – we should ask her at a time when she is likely to say 'Yes'. This is when her enthusiasm is high – in Figure 9.6 at point 1 or 2 and not point 3 a month later when her interest has died down.

Keep contact

When we have seen others in the decision-making process we need to feed back information to the initial contact and take the opportunity to remind her of the benefits we can bring.

Demonstrate that we are showing interest

If the time elapsing is fairly long we can sustain interest by cutting out and sending articles and information which would interest her, even if they are not directly relevant to our area of expertise.

Agree the contact frequency

Many professionals are afraid of 'pestering' prospects, so they go to the other extreme and let these contacts drift. This can easily be avoided by *agreeing* the frequency of contact with the prospect. Remember: we must have this discussion at a point where the 'interest curve' is high. We should also make the responsibility for making the contact ours, not hers.

Test commitment

As well as building commitment we should be checking it. It is easy to be deluded by polite prospects who make us feel better by projecting more enthusiasm than they feel. As discussed in Chapter 8, commitment involves the client in action. We can ask her to do something which will take a little time – e.g. send you some information – and if it does not arrive, question what interest really exists.

Involve the prospect in developing the need

See below.

Involve the prospect in the design and presentation of the solution

See below.

We hear of many more ways of sustaining enthusiasm used by professionals each day. The key is to understand that this is the aim of this part of the campaign and then to do anything to keep that curve going up.

Getting the timing right

There is a natural tendency in many of us either to move too quickly when there is a large prize in sight or alternatively to show how service-orientated we are by responding with solutions at the earliest possible time. If we succumb to these instincts we put ourselves at a disadvantage.

Figure 9.7 represents a situation where there is a time lag between first contact with a prospect and a decision to buy a specific service.

In this situation the right time to put forward our solutions is as close to decision date as possible, e.g. at point 1. Note: this assumes we have explored the commercial funnels and that we *know* the final decision date.

Figure 9.7: Timing our proposals

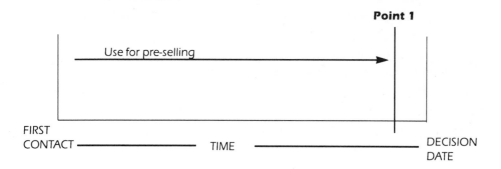

Why so late?

- If we put forward our ideas earlier the prospect can pass them on to others to see if they can do them more cheaply and she can also consider doing the work in-house.

- Alternatively if we give ourselves more time for gaining a comprehensive understanding of the requirements, issues and politics of the situation the solution is more likely to be right *and* acceptable to all.

- If we have some radical, and positive, ideas which change the situation materially the tendency is to communicate them to the prospect as soon as we think of them. This enables them to be passed on and tried out by others. However, if the prospect hears these radical ideas within a day or two of the decision date she has to decide in favour of our solution if she wants the benefits which these ideas deliver. This is especially powerful if we are trying to 'pull the rug' from underneath an incumbent firm.

- The more time we have between first contact and proposal the more time we have for 'pre-selling' and credibility building.

What is pre-selling?

In many competitive situations the people in the decision-making process have almost made up their minds who they will choose before they see the presentations or proposals! They know who they want to win and as long as that firm puts forward a credible solution in line with their expectations they will vote for them. The other competitors are there to make up numbers.

This does not mean that the presentation or proposal should not be first class. What it does mean is that we should ensure that our proposition is the one they are looking forward to and expecting to win. To this end we should invest as much energy as possible in the pre-selling phase, building up credibility and persuading the relevant people that we are the organisation they will want to work with.

David Maister in his article 'How Clients Choose' supports our conclusions. He says:

The vast majority of professional projects are awarded at the pre-proposal stage: the formal proposal and/or presentation merely confirm (or destroy) a decision already made. If you can't afford to spend time up-front, don't bother writing the proposal.

There are a number of actions we can take to develop credibility, build compatibility, demonstrate competence and place us in a strong tactical position in the month, quarter or even six months between first contact and final presentation of the solution. For example we can:

- Ensure we meet with all of the people who will have influence on the future decision.

- Introduce some new ideas which could become an integral part of the required solution. In this way we are changing the position of the goalposts for the other competitors. They will have to play 'catch up' – if they ever find out the goalposts have been moved.

- Try to find out the parts of competitors' solutions which are favoured – on the basis that some competitors will be tactically naive and submit proposals far too early.

- Build alliances with third parties who may be able to offer help.

- Invite key players from the prospective client to suitable hospitality events.

- Carry out 'mini assignments' and 'health checks' where we can demonstrate expertise very quickly.

- Invite the prospect to seminars where we can show our expertise and where she can meet our delighted clients.

- Send articles and information related to her situation which underline our knowledge.

- Invite her to our offices where she can meet a selection of people who are primed to say those things which will increase our credibility.

- If appropriate invite her to speak to relevant clients and possibly to meet them to see what benefits we have been able to bring to their organisations.

- Provide case studies of similar projects we have carried out.

- Introduce those people from our side who will actually carry out the work.

- Ensure that deadlines are agreed for any correspondence, contact etc. and that they are always met.

- Underpromise and overdeliver – promise to do things in an acceptable timescale and quality and then do better *every time*.

Pre-selling is *not* selling our solution. It is preparing the ground for a positive response. There is no point in spending considerable time and money on the best presentation or proposal unless we are prepared to invest the time in pre-selling. Delaying the final solution to the right point gives us the time to do this.

Developing the need

The PACES process makes it clear that the time and skill invested in understanding a client's requirements through effective funnelling forms the basis of a successful sale. It is true also that being 'funnelled' helps the client to consider her own perceived needs, real needs and wants more deeply.

To win significant new prospects the professional must ensure that all the key members involved in the decision-making process have been through this degree of 'soul searching'. They must not only understand the perceived needs. They must also understand:

- The real needs (if at variance to the perceived needs).
- The wider implications.
- The short- and long-term effects.
- The wants of people which may also have to be met.
- The effects on others.
- The relationship to corporate and departmental business objectives.
- The implications if things go wrong, are delayed, incomplete etc.
- The relative importance of each element of the needs.
- The specific elements of the professional's expertise which are critical to the success of the assignment.

If these elements are not understood in some depth by the key people within the client, they will believe that the need is very 'simple' and relatively easy to meet. This will mean that, in the prospect's eyes, a large number of firms could meet the need adequately and the services being considered will tend to be regarded as a commodity. This is how audit work is perceived now – with the obvious effect on profitability. Many accountants are attempting to 'bolt added value' onto audits in the hope of differentiating themselves and generating more profit. This will only be successful if each prospect can be helped to see the need for these extra services and to understand the wider implications of their purchasing decisions.

It follows from the above that we should spend considerable time with decision-makers and influencers getting them to understand their requirements. As discussed in earlier chapters, the fatal mistake is to try to *tell* the client what she needs, even if we are sure what we want her to think. The only way to help her to understand is by asking searching questions from a position of high credibility and demonstrable competence and compatibility.

The ideal outcome is for us (and the prospect) to understand the detailed requirements better than our competitors. However, even if the prospect communicates her new-found insight to our competition, we are still ahead because:

- We have already added value to the prospect.

- We have developed credibility and been involved in a consultant/client relationship rather than as buyer/seller (although as yet unpaid!).

- The 'specification' as developed is likely to have our 'fingerprints' all over it.

- With the requirements now being more demanding there are fewer competitors who will be able to put forward a credible solution.

Finally, defining the need in greater depth and avoiding a 'too simple' solution will help to ensure that the prospect gets the *right* solution – one that meets her needs most closely and provides the best short- and long-term benefits. Too often prospects buy what is 'easy to buy' and regret the decision at their leisure. If we are the winners in one of these situations we may not enjoy the resulting experience and the project will almost certainly not generate the level of benefits which will help us to win more business or generate referrals.

Measuring progress

'The project is worth £200,000 and the probability of us winning is 70 per cent.' Statements like this are heard in many professional firms, often with the following limitations:

- The 70 per cent probability is pure 'gut feel'.

- The £200,000 is guesswork and usually overstated.

- The professional's estimates are not reviewed later to measure their accuracy.

- This estimate is added together with other 'gut feels' to arrive at a forecast which appears now to be very scientific.

- The focus of the discussion is on the 70 per cent supposedly achieved and not on the 30 per cent gap which needs to be filled.

We have yet to find the perfect system which accurately measures the probability of winning business, especially if a relatively small number of large projects are being pursued.

However, the most important use of an accurate analysis is not to determine 'where we are' but is to aid in planning ACTIONS which will measurably reduce the gap, increase the probability figure and ultimately enable us to win the business.

The best way of measuring progress and planning forward movement is to divide the P3 Segment of the PACE Pipeline itself into four levels – Q1 to Q4. For a prospective piece of work to reach each level progress needs to have been made and a certain number of driving questions answered. These criteria and questions need to be very tough so that:

- They give a hard-nosed view on how far we have come.

- It is very clear what the next set of actions should be.

An example of such a framework is given below:

Table 9.2: Tracking progress (DMP = Decision-making Process; USP = Unique Selling Point; BOD = Basis of Decision)

Class	Qualification criteria	The driving questions
Qualified opportunity Level 1 **Q1**	1. Opportunity identified. 2. Discussions initiated.	Have we met with at least one person who has sufficient authority to give us a clear brief of requirements?
	3. Our solution possible.	Do we know that there is a problem or opportunity (agreed by the prospect) which needs resolution? Can we address the requirements? Is our solution likely to be technically acceptable?
	4. Our type of client.	Is the prospect likely to be willing to pay for the added value areas which we typically incorporate in our solutions?
Qualified opportunity Level 2 **Q2**	1. Bases of decision understood.	Do we fully understand their current situation (e.g. structure, processes, applications, incumbent systems)?
	2. Business drivers understood.	Do we fully understand the positioning and synergy of the incumbent suppliers?
	3. Budget situation understood.	Do we know the opportunity costs of their current situation?
	4. Players, timescales and DMP understood.	As a departmental objective, how important is this project? Why?
	5. Pre-selling strategy and plan formulated.	As a corporate objective, how important is the project? Why? Do we understand the financial operations of this company? Do they have the money available? Which budget does this come from? Is the budget sufficient to cover our solution? Who is the budget-holder? Could more money be found? If so, from where? Do we know all of the players in the DMP? Who are they? Have we met them? Do we know what their roles will be? Do we know the process by which this decision will be reached? What is this? Do we know the requirements of all of the players? Has the decision-maker committed to make a decision? Do we know their timescales for agreement and implementation? Have we formulated a strategy to pursue this prospect and have we put together a pre-selling plan?

Class	Qualification criteria	The driving questions
Qualified opportunity Level 3 **Q3**	1. Short-listed competitors know.	Have we presented a solution which has been cost-justified?
	2. Financially acceptable solution.	Has the prospect dedicated time/effort/resource to fully evaluate our solution? How has this been carried out?
	3. Talking with decision-maker and key influencers.	Has the solution been accepted and agreed by all the key players?
		Have the key players told us that they particularly like aspects of our solution? What are these aspects?
		Do we know all of the other alternatives they are considering?
		Are there no more than two other competitors still in the race?
		Do we know the offerings being made by the competitors?
		Have we created a requirement for USPs which only we can provide?
		Have our competition created a requirement for USPs which we will find difficult/impossible to provide?
		Have we got alternatives/arguments to deflect the competitors' USPs?
		If our proposal is accepted, what may the different individuals involved in the DMP have to give up?
Qualified opportunity Level 4 **Q4**	1. Verbal commitment.	Have we met the BOD of all the key players?
	2. 'Closing meeting' fixed.	Are we in a 'short list of one' with the business only subject to discussion and negotiation on final details?
	3. Paper trail understood.	
		Have we actually been told by the decision-maker (or his direct messenger) that we have won the business?
		Is a 'closing meeting' arranged?
		Do we understand, in detail, the client's paper trail – how, when, where and by whom the decision will be ratified from their side?
		Have we triggered the client's internal mechanism for raising a purchase agreement?
		Have we developed a genuine ally?

Applying this approach to live prospects and projects in the Pipeline often leads to a number of reactions:

- Surprise at how many 70 per cent prospects are still in Q1.

- Surprise at how few prospects are in Q3 or Q4.

- Concern at the number of absolutely critical questions we do not have a completely rock solid answer to.

By using this process one of our clients has managed to achieve an 80+ per cent conversion rate on opportunities moving between P3 and P4 of the Pipeline.

Proposal tactics

Introduction

The formal written proposal is an important part of the sales process. The ability to develop winning proposals is becoming crucial, particularly for those who find it difficult to differentiate their products, services or 'offering' in the mind of the client. However, the proposal itself is only one element of the process of 'winning'. Another equally important aspect is the ability to use proposals effectively.

Proposals and the sales cycle

By the time a client has decided that they need a proposal from us (and perhaps the competition) they have already identified some kind of problem – or opportunity – that needs resolution. Therefore, in many cases we are already very late in the sales process.

If we can identify the prospect's problem before they do, we give ourselves the opportunity of providing our solution without the constraints that competition and alternatives often generate. Therefore we should be working with prospects to ensure that we spot problems and opportunities before they occur rather than responding to the known. We should be trying to create an edge for ourselves by approaching prospects with new ideas before their existing advisers identify them. This often highlights to the client where their existing adviser relationship has become too familiar and where they are not getting added value.

Proposals – do they really want one?

Often prospective clients ask for a proposal, 'because that's the thing to do'. If asked to provide a proposal, we need to ensure that is what the client really wants. Often this is the only mechanism they recognise to help them to make a decision. In fact research shows that competitive proposals and their follow-up often confuse the decision to be made rather than simplifying it. We should offer alternatives to a proposal that might give us an advantage. For example:

- A visit to our offices to allow the client to see and experience the unique features/ approach that only we have to offer.

- A visit to see an already happy client, who will undertake some of the selling for us.

- A presentation with plenty of interaction, thus allowing us to adapt our proposals more closely to the client's requirements, as we go.

- A 'workshop' involving the client's decision-making team designed to stimulate plenty of discussion again allowing us to adapt our proposals more closely to the client's requirements.

Before offering alternatives we should consider those areas in which we and our organisation have particular expertise. We can then build our alternative to a proposal around those strengths. This may be the only real way to differentiate ourselves from the competition.

Proposals – keeping the prospect involved

Once we have gained the opportunity to prepare a proposal, we must not retreat to our 'ivory tower' and leave the prospective client alone until it is completed. If we can ensure that the prospect's interest is stimulated during this period we have a far better chance of winning the business.

Before starting work on the proposal, we should ask the client if it is acceptable to contact her with any questions and queries that may arise. We should then plan to do so. If there is a delay between gaining the opportunity and completion of the proposal then we must phone the client, ask questions to clarify details and tell her how the proposal is developing.

Before producing the finished article it is generally a very good tactic to produce a draft copy (marked clearly DRAFT COPY), and then arrange a meeting with the client. At this meeting we should stress that we have a draft copy of the proposal and that we would like their input. One copy is enough. This ensures that both sides have to 'get together' to study the draft. Based upon our information-gathering meetings we should select the areas that were of greatest interest to the client. We then ask for her comments 'to ensure that we have understood absolutely correctly'. If she has any observations we should suggest that she makes her comments directly onto the draft proposal. All of this helps to make it *her* proposal not ours. If this is the case then at final proposal stage she will be looking for ways to agree with our recommendations, not to pick holes in them.

We can then make arrangements with the client to hand-deliver the final proposal, to give us the opportunity to answer any queries she may have. This creates an additional opportunity for us to develop our ideas further and is particularly useful when our proposal is the last to arrive with the client.

If there is to be a delay between giving the proposal to the client and her making a decision, we can ask for approval to 'keep in touch' during this period – and make sure that we do – but don't push!

The proposal itself

The main elements of the proposal are normally:

- The people to be involved.

- Understanding of their business.

- The proposed service / solution.

- Our company and why they should choose us.

The people

Selection of the right team is essential. Ideally, these should be people who have already worked together and who will create the image of a team. If not, the process of working on a major proposal should be used to develop this team cohesion quickly. To the prospective client, the people may well be the biggest single differentiating factor. They should spend as much time as possible with the prospect.

Understanding the business

Perceptive identification of issues the prospect is facing, is impressive. The real challenge is to identify these issues (without merely parroting the prospect's comments) and demonstrate how our proposal will address them to the target's benefit.

Identification of themes which will 'turn on' the prospect and opportunities to add value by addressing them is crucial. This relies on:

- Understanding the industry and market developments.

- Understanding the prospective client's business and competition.

- Awareness of current business issues.

The best strategy is to add value in the proposal process. This may not be in the document itself. Delivering suggestions, writing separate letters or introducing relevant experts may be more productive. If we cannot add value at once we should at least demonstrate how we will bring benefits in future, perhaps by using specific examples from other clients.

The service / solution

Our research shows that companies are looking for:

- Responsive, accessible, personal service.

- Commitment to their interests.

- Proactivity.

- Pragmatism.

- Value for money.

They tend to complain of:

- Confrontational or technically oriented attitudes.
- Inadequate co-ordination of a range of services.
- Lack of staff continuity.
- Fees / price.

The listing of other clients with similar characteristics to the prospect is conventional but is rarely a differentiating factor. It is more impressive to:

- Demonstrate instances of specific projects relevant to the prospect.
- Give favourable quotes from clients.
- Offer clients as references.

Our company

Points to remember are:

- As with other aspects of the proposal, our major competitors can offer almost anything we can to a high standard.
- Simply to claim wider coverage or experience, whether of geography, industry or discipline, will not in itself differentiate us.
- Claims must be matched to the prospect's requirements and convincingly demonstrated.
- Size in itself is rarely a positive sales feature and can be off-putting.

Research

Good research is vital to conveying the correct messages of industry and client knowledge. We have access to a wide range of published sources and these should be used to the full, together with any in-house analytical ability and specialists. Documents such as sales brochures are often particularly informative both about a prospective client's business, culture and concerns.

Professionalism

To claim to be more professional than the competition creates little impact. To demonstrate it by impeccable organisation and administration is impressive. Examples are:

- Being excellently briefed.
- Being always available by telephone. We should consider giving the client a help line on which she can always reach a member of the team.
- Agreeing to the prospect's suggested times for meetings.
- Beginning (and ending) meetings on time.
- Submitting well-thought-out agendas in advance.

- Confirming arrangements by letter.

- Thanking for assistance and conveying information in writing by return of post.

- Getting names, titles and addresses exactly right.

Fee handling

Price versus value

In most competitive situations the fee will be a key element in the prospect's decision to buy. However, unless our service is a pure commodity, where the only difference between competitors is price, the prospect will be making a judgement concerning price and value. While the price needs to be competitive, our real efforts need to go into building value in the eyes of the client.

When to present the price

Timing is important. Everything mentioned so far in this section has been focused on increasing the prospect's motivation to buy and building her perceived value of what we do. If we are tempted – or forced – into presenting our fees before this motivation is built, the prospect may immediately dismiss us as 'too expensive'. If, however, the prospect has been so impressed by our approach, our solution and the benefits of our proposals that she starts to believe she 'cannot live without our services' *before we discuss fees* she will be looking for ways of justifying the price. The message is: delay presenting the price until the prospect wants to buy.

It is important to note the difference between *price* and *budget*. Price comes towards the end of the process. Budget is a factor we need to find out as early as possible so that we can tailor our solution to meet the prospect's pocket.

Determining value

The value the client puts on our solution will depend on:

- The importance of the 'problem'.

- The benefits which derive from the solution.

- The urgency of the need.

- The number and quality of potential alternative suppliers.

- The corporate and personal implications of getting the project right or wrong.

How we price our work should take these factors into account. We need to establish the answers to these questions (and influence the prospective client's views) during the A and C phases of the PACES process.

Believing our pricing

The price we get will also be determined by how much *we believe* we, or our solution, are worth. Two weeks before an important pitch we were observing a team of consultants preparing their presentations. When it got to discussing the fees one said,

'That looks expensive, don't you remember we lost the last one at this rate.' There was a general murmur of agreement but the partner present said: 'No – we need this fee to make this project worthwhile.' It was obvious that no one was convinced. This was not only obvious to us but also to the prospect the week after.

The person responsible for presenting the price element of the presentation hesitated, shuffled, mumbled a little and lost eye contact with the prospective clients at that precise point for the first time during the presentation. The prospects, consciously or subconsciously noted these signals and one immediately commented, 'That sounds expensive.' After the presentation the initial doubter said, 'Told you so!' He could not see that it was his own lack of confidence, which came across very clearly, that stimulated the prospect's response in the first place. It was a classic 'self-fulfilling prophecy'.

This attitude is central to the profitable success of a professional who has a 'product' which may be invisible and where there is no set price. In this situation we have noticed that a major factor in deciding the rate which can be achieved is the professional's own confidence in what the solution is 'worth'. This confidence must be built. The seller needs to be convinced before the buyer can be.

It should therefore be clear that the issue of price handling is not an issue in isolation. A professional who skilfully follows the path described in this book will build value in the eyes of the prospect and in his own mind. This professional will command higher rates.

Handling fee resistance

We know professionals who send in proposals to prospective clients and then wait to hear whether they have won or lost. In some selling environments there is no alternative to this. In many others, however, it is possible to have some contact with the prospect after she has examined the proposals and before she has made the decision. This gives the seller the chance to explore and handle any issues which are not exactly right. One of these issues might be the fees.

We would suggest that if it is possible to have some discussion before the decision is made then this chance must be grasped. That is not to say that we will automatically reduce the price but it does mean that if there is a 'deal' which is acceptable to both sides it can be found.

However, this situation must be handled well. It is probably the part of the process where instinct is the poorest guide. When someone says 'You're too expensive!' there are two instinctive reactions: either we start to mumble and reduce the rate easily, or we defend our rates mightily.

The latter of these sounds more productive but not if it is done like this:

Prospect   You're too expensive!

Professional   Well Ms Prospect, not when you consider what you are getting for your money. We are providing top quality staff and an excellent project manager. The technology we are using is state of the art and our people will be providing very detailed reports at each stage. I have asked our Director to take a personal interest and I will be involved on a day-to-day basis. Also . . .

The danger here is that the professional has started to include features which are not relevant to the client, certainly are not valuable and are only included now to defend the fee. In effect the professional is confirming the prospect's views – these unwanted features explain *why* he is too expensive. This is absolutely the wrong way to handle fee resistance.

When the prospect states we are too expensive we need to find out more:

- What is she comparing us to?
- What are the details of the competitive offers (as known by the prospect)? In particular have they scoped the project in the same way or built in more reliance on scarce client resources?
- What are the competing rates?

This information may be hard to ascertain but:

- The more the prospect wants us to win the more open she will be.
- The more allies we have in the prospect organisation the more sources of information we have.
- The more we gather and share competitor information the better we are able to estimate their rates – if necessary.
- There is much less risk in asking than in not asking.

Once we have some idea of the difference in price and the difference in solutions between us and each of the variable solutions we can do the only thing possible – sell our extra benefits for the extra price we are asking. We should not resell benefits that are common to a number of alternatives – the prospect's response will be: 'I can get all that elsewhere and spend less.' We must focus on the difference.

If the extra benefits we are offering are not worth the extra price then the prospect should buy from the competition! There is no magic wand!

However, we should consider two factors:

1. We do not have to *be* better – the prospect just needs to *think* we are. For instance if we know the competitor has everything we have to offer but their professional is poor at selling, we may still be able to convince the client of the added advantages in choosing us – and also achieve a fee premium.

2. Our extra benefits may not be worth all of the proposed difference to the client but they may be worth a proportion. In this instance it may be necessary for us to negotiate a reduction in rates but not right down to the competitor's rate. As all business managers know, the small percentages saved here add up.

Summary

Price is always likely to be an important factor in the client's decision. Our challenge is to build the value of our solution in the prospect's mind so that the potential cost of not using us outweighs any premium we can charge. This value derives from using every skill and tactic described in this book so far. If a professional is effective at selling in a consultative fashion he will not only generate more business – he will also achieve higher fee rates than others in the same profession who are less skilful or less confident.

And if we can achieve higher rates we don't have to work so hard for the same return!

Presentation tactics

Many professional firms have spent considerable amounts of money in recent years in developing their senior people's presentation skills. It seemed the obvious first step when the marketplace became more competitive and clients were arranging formal pitches and 'beauty parades' as part of the purchasing process. It should be clear from this book that the presentation is only one link in the chain and, while it is important to be able to present well, the most polished speakers will not necessarily secure the client.

Before standing up to make a pitch to one or more decision-makers and influencers the successful professional will have achieved as many of the following as humanly possible. He will have:

- Explored all of the issues (technical, business, commercial and personal).

- Built credibility with all of the key people present.

- Developed the need and helped to write the specification.

- Tested his solutions and gained input from the decision-makers so that these solutions are as much theirs as his.

- Understood the decision-making process and found out what each person will want to hear.

- Focused on the areas where his firm has an advantage over the competition. This information will be gleaned from the decision-makers themselves or his 'allies' in the prospect.

- Checked his understanding of the real situation through his intelligence network in the prospect.

- Focused on the issues which are closest to the hearts of the people with real INFLUENCE both in the organisation and with regard to this decision.

- Prepared the ground so that the audience are keen to hear the presentation and *expect* it to be the best.

Once we are in this position *then* we should focus on presenting well. We should also employ the tactics that ensure we will win.

What tactics can we use?

Try to meet everyone beforehand

Ideally meet everyone beforehand – or at least the key decision influencers.

On the positive side this allows us to personalise the presentation to the individuals present. For instance:

> 'Fred, your key interest was in the communication process throughout the project – what we have done here is . . .
>
> . . . while for you Joe the critical issue was in the person you would be working directly with – we would propose George because he has . . .
>
> . . . Jane, while the areas I have covered are also very important for you, the most important consideration for your department is on Health and Safety, our plans here are . . . etc.'

A presentation should sound like a conversation with the audience. If we have not met them before, this is very hard to achieve.

On the negative side we have seen the risks at first hand of *not* meeting with *all* of the key people before the presentation. In one instance we took a training brief from the Human Resources Director of a major plc – it was quite detailed and we felt we had a very credible solution. The presentation was to the Human Resources Director, Managing Director and Sales Director. As usual we started the presentation by summarising our understanding of the requirements. Half-way through the summary the Managing Director became restless and by the end her body language was positively hostile. We tried to find out why:

Us	Jane, you don't appear too happy – is anything not correct in the summary?
Jane	Nothing is correct. It's all wrong. That's not the situation and it's not what I came along here today to see.
Us	Which bits are you not happy about?
Jane	All of it – you clearly do not understand the issues.
Us	Alison (the Human Resources Director) – I'm sure these were the areas we discussed in some detail. Has anything changed since our last meeting?
Alison	(Backtracking madly) Oh no – I would agree with the Managing Director – I am afraid you must have misinterpreted what I said.
Us	Gulp!!

As you can imagine we did not secure the client!

Make it different

Think of different ways to present the solution. Personalise it to the client. If it is a high-tech prospect make it high tech. If it is a newspaper company, present the message as 'news'. If it is a publishing company, produce a 'magazine'.

We have seen beauty parades where accountants spend most of their time convincing the prospect that they know how to carry out an audit and lawyers who focus on convincing the client they know the law. The clients afterwards complained that they could not tell the difference between the firms presenting and what they wanted to hear was anything special in terms of service, people, 'delivery' or added value. Make it different – the most important thing is to be remembered.

Go last

Much research shows this is the best position for most circumstances. If we go last and demonstrate real effectiveness we have the best chance of being remembered. Engineer the situation by finding out when the last slot is and then plead for as much time as possible to 'get the presentation exactly right'.

If we can't go last, go first

If we are presenting first we should think up one or two very difficult questions that all the presenting firms could be asked. Spend time thinking of the best answers to these questions. If at the end of the presentation the questions have not been asked we should bring them up ourselves by saying, 'One question you may be asking yourself at this point might be . . . the way we would handle this would be . . .'

The prospect is now very likely to ask this question of all of our competitors. Unlike us they only have a couple of seconds to think of a good answer. In effect we will have laid one or more time bombs to go off in our competitors' faces! Remember we are playing to win!

Practise and rehearse

Everyone knows the difference a rehearsal can make to the quality of a presentation – especially if more than one person is involved. We would recommend two or three rehearsals to get it right.

We would also recommend rehearsing the presentation *with the client!* Why would she agree to that? One very good reason is that if one or more people are responsible for organising the beauty parade then their credibility is at stake as much as ours – they are keen to 'get it right'. In that instance, and if we have developed a reasonable relationship with the person, we should ask whether we can 'run through what we are going to say just to make sure we have got it spot on'. (If we cannot arrange a meeting a ten-minute phone call could be invaluable.)

Our reward comes when our contact says: 'It sounds good, just two points – I think you should stress your experience with ABC Ltd a bit more – the Managing Director really admires them – and, whatever you do, reduce the "technospeak" at the beginning, that would put the Sales Director right off and he won't listen to the rest.' These tips will often mean the difference between success and failure.

Two final points:

- We might as well ask if we can rehearse with the client – there is nothing to lose.

- Ensure we are talking with an accurate and well-informed source – remember Alison, the Human Resources Director mentioned earlier!

STRATEGIES WHICH WIN NEW CLIENTS – SUMMARY

Winning significant new clients means achieving a balance between thought and action. It means deciding what is best, and then carrying out the appropriate plan rather than believing that hard work alone will bring the right level of reward.

To be successful the professional firm should:

- concentrate its firepower on the right targets based on timely and accurate intelligence;

- identify, meet and influence the right people in each situation;

- plan, carry out and review the tactics at each stage of the buying process to ensure that the firm wins.

If this seems like a lot of effort – it can be. Whether it is appropriate depends on one question: 'What is/will be the "lifetime value" of this prospect as a client?'

Chapter 10 **Some Final Thoughts**

What This Book Can and Cannot Do

HOW TO BECOME A GREAT PERFORMER

There are two steps to effectively developing any skill to a high level. The learner has to first of all understand what it is that he is trying to achieve – someone has to delineate the skill. As a novice golfer this could be achieved by reading a book on how to improve our swing. Looking at the illustrations would help. A video would be useful. Having a golf pro demonstrate and talk us through the various parts of the swing would be even more useful. This person could answer our specific questions.

However, none of this learning will, by itself, improve our swing.

What we need is a second stage to the learning process. We must practise and get useful feedback. This involves hours on the driving range and putting greens. It involves spending money on more lessons.

The best sports people practise and train constantly. They know what they want to achieve and training is the process which gets them closer and closer to the levels of achievement they seek. All top international golf and tennis players today have personal coaches – people skilled in training and giving feedback.

Sport is not the only analogy. It is the same for any skill. Top musicians practise for hours each day. Mechanics working for racing teams are individuals who were willing to learn, practise and train to become the top exponents in their field.

Serious training and practice are not essential if we are prepared to play the game purely for enjoyment. However, our match results will mostly read as losses. This may not matter to the social golfer but in business it is a philosophy which does not stand well in the competitive markets of the twenty-first century.

Will you apply these winning processes and skills?

In this book we have provided the reader with a step-by-step approach to creating new clients. We have tried to be meticulous in the level of detail we have provided – not just stating what needs to be done but also giving illustrations of how it can be done. We have delineated the skill clearly.

The caveat is probably obvious. Reading this book and then doing no more will not result in anyone becoming a better seller or marketeer. Training, practice and feedback will also be needed to translate the messages of this book into effective behaviour.

Obvious as this message may be, professionals are prone to overlooking this.

One reason is that they tend to be locked in by their own experience. For most professionals a great deal of their learning has come from reading books and listening to the pro. To develop the knowledge and understanding of the processes which underpin their profession this is a perfectly suitable method of learning.

Learning to use a skill is a different process.

Also, because professionals (rightly) value their time, this can translate into an unwillingness to devote time to new learning. We frequently receive requests to speak for an hour at a meeting or to run a brief after-hours training session.

The implicit assumption is that whilst it takes years to qualify as a top professional, one can learn to become a top salesperson or marketeer in the lunch hour! Professional salespeople who have spent their careers working to become more successful and who regularly earn six-figure incomes as a result of their capabilities with customers would find this concept laughable.

In this book we have sought to provide answers. We conclude with a question and a suggestion.

What will you do to incorporate all of the ideas, practices and skills contained in this book (which you do not apply today) in order for them to become 'normal' practice in your way of working?

The gap may be large – it may seem like attempting to eat an elephant. However, the solution to eating an elephant has been around for a long time. There is only one way to eat an elephant – bit by bit.

Pick a couple of ideas from this book that you believe will have immediate positive impact and begin application right away. Once these are working for you, take another and then another.

Choose small changes in behaviour which will lead to success. With success comes positive feelings and changed attitudes. With positive feelings and the right attitude the next step of implementation is so much easier and consequently more effective.

Just do *something* today!

Index